EVERYDAY KOREAN IDIOMATIC EXPRESSIONS

100 Expressions You Can't Live Without

EVERYDAY KOREAN IDIOMATIC EXPRESSIONS

한국에서 자주 쓰이는 관용 표현 100가지

1판 1쇄	1st edition published	2014. 1. 13.
개정판 1쇄	1st revised edition published	2025. 5. 12.

지은이	Written by	Talk To Me In Korean
책임편집	Edited by	안효진 Hyojin An, 스테파니 베이츠 Stephanie Bates
디자인	Design by	김민재 Minjae Kim
삽화	Illustration by	김경해 Kyounghae Kim
펴낸곳	Published by	롱테일북스 Longtail Books
펴낸이	Publisher	이수영 Suyoung Lee
편집	Copy-edited by	김보경 Florence Kim
주소	Address	04033 서울특별시 마포구 양화로 113, 3층(서교동, 순흥빌딩)
		3rd Floor, 113 Yanghwa-ro, Mapo-gu, Seoul, KOREA
이메일	E-mail	editor@ltinc.net
ISBN		978-1-942791-63-8 13710

TTMIK - TALK TO ME IN KOREAN

한국에서 자주 쓰이는
관용 표현 100가지

Written by
Talk To Me In Korean

EVERYDAY KOREAN IDIOMATIC EXPRESSIONS

100 Expressions You Can't Live Without

CONTENTS

HOW TO USE
EVERYDAY KOREAN IDIOMATIC EXPRESSIONS

Nearly every language in the world has idiomatic expressions which can be difficult to decipher at first. For example, in American English, "it's raining cats and dogs" does not literally mean that cats or dogs are falling from the sky. Korean is no exception to this. If you have watched Korean TV shows or movies, or have engaged in conversation with people in Korean, you may have heard a few things that do not translate very well to other languages. This book has been designed to help you better understand those expressions and use them when you speak or write Korean.

Sometimes these idiomatic expressions can be used on their own, but they are often used as part of a longer sentence, depending on the context. First, make sure you understand the meaning of a certain expression by reading the description and looking at the illustrations. Second, check out the sample dialogues to see how it is actually used in context. Finally, once you fully understand that particular expression, we advise that you put your knowledge to the test by using it with a Korean speaker, in person or on the Internet, to make sure it sticks in your mind and to ensure that you are using it correctly.

Whether you are just beginning to learn Korean or you have the fluency of a native speaker, you can use this book however you'd like, but preferably not as a beverage coaster or a bathroom reader. Use it as a reference book to look up a phrase you recently heard but do not understand, or use to study each of the 100 expressions individually. You can also study numbers 1 through 100 sequentially, or open up to a random page each day to learn a new expression. Whichever way you choose to use this book, it is essential to improving your Korean skills and an excellent resource to have in your library.

100

CHAPTER. 1

뒤 = behind; back; rear
북 = drum
치다 = to hit, to strike;
to play (an instrument)

뒷북치다
[**dwit-ppuk-chi-da**]

LITERAL TRANSLATION:
to hit the back of the drum

ACTUAL USAGE:
to hear about something late (certain news);
to fuss around after the event

The idiomatic expression **뒷북치다** is used when someone learns about something after everyone else knows about it, but thinks it is new information or is something that just happened. If someone is rushing around belatedly or is making a big deal about something after it already happened, you can tell them, "**뒷북치지 마세요.**"

A: 그 소식 들었어요?

   B: 뭐요?

A: 선영 씨랑 우진 씨랑 사귄대요.

   B: 그걸 아직도 몰랐어요? 뒷북치지 말아요.

A: Did you hear the news?

   B: What?

A: Seonyeong and Woojin are dating.

   B: You didn't know that yet? Stop fussing around what everybody knows already.

A: 오늘 회사에서 회식하는 거 들었어요?

   B: 당연하죠. 전 지난주에 들었어요.

A: 진짜요? 그리고 내일은 일 안 한대요!

   B: 알고 있어요. 항상 뒷북치시네요.

A: Did you hear about the company dinner tonight?

   B: Of course. I heard about it last week.

A: Really? And we are not working tomorrow!

   B: I know. You're always one step behind.

CHAPTER. 2

둘 = two (native Korean number)
두 is the adjective form of 둘.
손 = hand
발 = foot
다 = all; every
들다 = to raise

두 손 두 발 다 들다

[du son du bal da deul-da]

LITERAL TRANSLATION:
to raise one's both hands and both feet

ACTUAL USAGE:
to give up on a person

This expression is used when you want to express that you are throwing your hands up in despair because someone is not meeting your expectations or you cannot change his/her mind or behavior no matter how hard you try. It is most commonly used when you are giving up on or losing hope about someone. The expression can also be used when someone is too passionate about something and you cannot stop him/her from doing it.

A: 한국어 공부 왜 안 해?

   B: 요즘 일이 바빠서 시간이 없어.

A: 한국어 공부는 매일 해야 해.

   B: 내일 할 거야. 진짜 바빴어.

A: 매일 한다고 말만 하고 바쁘다고 핑계만 대고. 아휴... 내가 두 손 두 발 다 들었다.

A: Why are you not studying Korean?

   B: I'm busy with work these days, so I don't have time.

A: You have to study Korean every day.

   B: I will study tomorrow. I've been really busy.

A: You only keep saying that you'll do it tomorrow and giving excuses... (Sigh) I give up!

A: 제가 부탁한 거 다 했어요?

   B: 아... 미안해요. 깜빡했어요. 내일 꼭 할게요.

A: 또요? 이거 제가 한 달 전에 부탁한 거예요.

   B: 벌써 한 달이나 됐어요? 진짜 내일 할게요.

A: 됐어요. 전 현준 씨한테 두 손 두 발 다 들었어요.

A: Did you finish what I asked you to do?

   B: Oh, I'm sorry. I forgot. I promise I'll do it tomorrow for sure.

A: Again? I asked you to do this a month ago.

   B: It's already been a month? I'll really do it tomorrow.

A: Forget about it. I give up on you, Hyeonjun.

CHAPTER. 3

아직 = (not) yet
멀다 = to be far

아직 멀었어요

[a-jik meo-reo-sseo-yo]

LITERAL TRANSLATION:

it is still far away

ACTUAL USAGE:

to still have a long way to go
(project, work, one's skill, distance),
it won't happen anytime soon
(time)

아직 멀었어요 is almost always used in the past tense, even when referring to something happening in the present. It can also be used when you receive a compliment and you want to sound humble, such as in "아니에요, 아직 멀었어요" ("No, I still have a long way to go"). A similar expression is "아직 잘 못해요" ("I'm still not good at it yet").

A: 우와, 이 의자 태수 씨가 직접 만들었어요?
B: 네. 제가 직접 만들었어요. 어때요?
A: 진짜 예뻐요. 팔아도 될 것 같아요.
B: 아니에요. 아직 멀었어요.

A: Wow. Taesu, did you make this chair yourself?
B: Yes, I made it myself. What do you think?
A: It's really pretty. I think you can go ahead and sell it.
B: No. I still have a long way to go.

A: 문준배 선수, 오늘도 홈런을 치셨어요.
B: 네, 운이 좋았어요.
A: 역시 아빠를 닮아 야구 실력이 뛰어나시네요.
B: 아니에요. 아빠 따라가려면 아직 멀었죠.

A: Joonbae Moon, you hit another home run today.
B: Yes, I was lucky.
A: You really inherited your father's excellent baseball skills.
B: No, I still have a long way to go to match my dad.

CHAPTER. 4

놀다 = to play; to hang out

놀고 있다
[**nol-go it-tta**]

LITERAL TRANSLATION:
to be playing, to be hanging out

ACTUAL USAGE:
to be not working at the moment;
what you're doing or saying is pathetic

놀고 있다 is the present participle form (-ing form) of 놀다, which means "to play," "to hang out," or "to have fun." 놀고 있다 can be used in two different ways: neutral and negative. In a neutral context, it is used to express that someone is doing the opposite of working, such as "playing around," "fooling around," "not working," "not focusing on what he/she has to do," or is "jobless." However, in a negative context, it is used when you are making fun of or laughing at someone for trying too hard to accomplish something, or the way they are going about it is meaningless and childish.

A: 지금 뭐 해?
　　B: 한국어 발음 연습해.
A: 근데 TV는 왜 켜 놨어?
　　B: 그냥 심심해서. TV 보면서 연습하고 있어.
A: 놀고 있다. 하나만 열심히 해.

A: What are you doing?
　　B: I'm practicing my Korean pronunciation.
A: Then why is the TV on?
　　B: I was just bored. I am practicing while watching TV.
A: Get out of here. Focus on one thing.

A: 노래방 가자.
　　B: 오늘도? 어제도 노래방 갔잖아.
A: 노래방 가서 연습해야 돼. 다음 달에 오디션 볼 거야.
　　B: 놀고 있네. 공부나 열심히 해.

A: Let's go to the singing room.
　　B: Again today? We went there yesterday, too.
A: I need to go practice in the singing room. I'm going to an audition next month.
　　B: Shut up. You just need to study.

CHAPTER. 5

뒤통수 = the back of one's head
치다 = to hit, to strike; to play (an instrument)

뒤통수치다
[**dwi-tong-su-chi-da**]

LITERAL TRANSLATION:
to strike the back of someone's head

ACTUAL USAGE:
to betray someone when they are off guard

The meaning of 뒤통수치다 originates from a situation similar to the English expression "backstabber" - imagine that you turned your back toward someone, thinking it was safe to do so, but that person hits you on the back of the head. You can use this expression when you describe a situation when a person betrays someone, but no one expected it.

A: 진수 선배 정말 친절한 것 같아요.

　　B: 왜? 너한테 잘해줘?

A: 네. 저한테 맛있는 것도 사주고 과제도 도와주고 그래요.

　　B: 진수 선배 조심해. 나중에 뒤통수친다는 소문이 있어.

A: I think Jinsu is really kind.

　　B: Why? Is he nice to you?

A: Yes. He buys me delicious foods and helps me with my homework.

　　B: Be careful with him. Rumor has it that he is a back-stabber.

A: 수연 씨, 요즘 회사 다니고 있어요?

　　B: 아니요. 취업하기 너무 힘들어요.

A: 그렇죠? 저랑 같이 카페 창업할래요?

　　B: 네? 사람들이 동업은 하면 안 좋다고 하던데...

A: 왜요? 제가 설마 수연 씨 뒤통수를 치겠어요?

A: Suyeon, are you working at a company these days?

　　B: No, it's difficult to get a job these days.

A: It is, right? Do you want to open a coffee shop with me?

　　B: What? People say it's not good to run a business together with someone.

A: Why? I wouldn't betray you, would I?

CHAPTER. 6

불난 데 부채질하다
[bul-lan de bu-chae-jil-ha-da]

LITERAL TRANSLATION:

to use a hand fan at the fire

ACTUAL USAGE:

fan the flame; to add fuel to the fire

This expression is derived from the action of building a fire: once the kindling is lit, the fire needs to spread in order to be useable. In order to make the fire larger, one must 1) blow onto the fire to make it spread, 2) use a fan to spread the flames, 3) pour gasoline onto a larger area. Sometimes, if there is too much wind or gasoline, the fire may become too big and cause damage. Idiomatically, "불난 데 부채질하다" refers to making a problem worse by talking about it or bringing it up. For example, a friend of yours recently broke up with his girlfriend and is trying to move on, but you keep bringing up the subject of the break up in an effort to comfort your friend. Your words of comfort are "fanning the flames" and actually making matters worse.

A: 아.. 주식이 또 떨어졌어... 아... 내 주식...

　　B: 지난번에 펀드 해서 손해 보더니 이번에는 주식이야?

A: 불난 데 부채질하지 말고 조용히 해.

A: Oh, my stocks have dropped again. My stocks...

　　B: You lost money by investing in some trust fund last time, and
　　　now it's stocks?

A: Don't add fuel to the fire and be quiet.

A: 지난 주말에 소개팅했는데 전화를 안 받아.

　　B: 소개팅 또 했어?

A: 응. 근데 오늘 전화했는데 전화를 안 받아. 왜 그러지?

　　B: 그 여자는 너가 싫은 거야. 너 소개팅만 하면 여자가
　　　항상 전화 안 받잖아.

A: 또 또... 불난 데 부채질한다.

A: I went on a blind date last weekend, but the girl is not answering my
　　phone calls.

　　B: You went on a blind date again?

A: Yeah, and I called her today, but she doesn't answer. Why is that?

　　B: She doesn't like you. Whenever you go on a blind date, the girl
　　　always avoids your calls.

A: You're doing it again...adding insult to injury.

CHAPTER. 7

입 = mouth
모으다 = to collect; to gather

입을 모으다
[**i-beul mo-eu-da**]

LITERAL TRANSLATION:
to gather mouths

ACTUAL USAGE:
many people have the same opinion
about something;
many people say the same thing

When two or more people are saying the same thing, or have the same opinion about something, they are collectively saying something as one voice. For example, **"사람들이 입을 모아서 이 웹사이트를 칭찬해요"** means that "everyone is saying nice things about this website."

A: 올해에는 경제 상황이 좀 좋아질까요?

　B: 글쎄요. 전문가들이 앞으로 2~3년은
　　계속 안 좋을 거라고 입을 모으던데요.

A: 그래요? 정말 걱정이네요.

A: Will the economic situation improve this year?

　B: I'm not sure. Experts seem to agree
　　that it will continue to be bad for the next 2 to 3 years.

A: Really? That's really concerning.

A: 너 요즘 사람들한테 이것저것 부탁하고 다닌다며?

　B: 내가? 아니야. 누가 그래?

A: 다들 입을 모아 말하더라.

A: I hear that you are asking people for favors here and there.

　B: Me? No. Who said that?

A: Everybody's saying that.

CHAPTER. 8

손 = hand
놓다 = to let something go

손 놓고 있다
[son no-ko it-tta]

LITERAL TRANSLATION:
to not have one's hands on something

ACTUAL USAGE:
to not do anything about something
that's supposed to be done

손 놓고 있다 implies a certain type of procrastination—not having the motivation to do something you know should be done or being at a loss as to what to do. It can also mean "to avoid doing something because it is stressful." However, the longer you put it off, the worse things become. For this situation, you can say "손 놓고 있었더니 일이 커졌어요."

A: 지난주에 준 프로젝트 다 끝났어요?

　　B: 아니요. 지금 우리 팀 모두 손 놓고 있어요.

A: 왜요?

　　B: 사장님이 다른 프로젝트를 먼저 하라고 해서요.

A: Is the project I gave you last week finished?

*　　B: No. The whole team is not working on it now.*

A: Why?

*　　B: Because the boss told us to work on another project first.*

A: 제 동생이 자꾸 사고를 쳐서 걱정이에요.

　　B: 아직도요? 말을 잘 해 봐요.

A: 말을 해도 안 들어요.

　　B: 그래도 손 놓고 있을 수는 없잖아요. 다시 한 번 잘 말해 보세요.

A: I am worried because my brother keeps getting into trouble.

*　　B: Still? Try and talk to him nicely.*

A: Even if I talk to him, he won't listen.

*　　B: But you can't procrastinate. Try and talk to him nicely once again.*

손 놓고 있다

CHAPTER. 9

번지수 = house number, street number
잘못 = in a wrong way
찾다 = to look for; to find

번지수를 잘못 찾다
[beon-ji-ssu-reul jal-mot chat-tta]

LITERAL TRANSLATION:
to have found the wrong house number

ACTUAL USAGE:
to ask for favor to someone
who wouldn't or can't do it for you

Imagine you need help from someone, so you ask for help, but this person cannot actually help you or does not want to. This situation is similar to when a letter or parcel is delivered to the wrong address; the item is there, but it's been sent to the wrong place. This expression can also be used when you've chosen the wrong person to deal with and they are dangerous or scary.

A: 돈 좀 빌려줘.

B: 나 돈 없는데...

A: 많다고 소문 났던데. 그러지 말고 좀 빌려줘.

B: 번지수 잘못 찾았어. 나 진짜 없어.

A: Lend me some money.

B: I don't have money.

A: Rumor has it that you have a lot of money. Please don't be like that and lend me some money.

B: You're barking up the wrong tree. I really don't have money.

A: 경진 씨, 오랜만이야. 잘 지냈어?

B: 잘 지내셨어요?

A: 경진 씨 부장으로 승진했다며? 우리 딸 취업 좀 시켜줘.

B: 번지수 잘못 찾으셨어요. 저희 회사 요즘 어려워서 있는 사람도 해고되고 있어요.

A: Kyeong-jin, long time no see. How have you been?

B: How have you been?

A: I heard you got promoted to manager. Please get my daughter a job.

B: You are barking up the wrong tree. My company is not doing well these days and even the current employees are being fired.

번지수를 잘못 찾다

CHAPTER. 10

말 = word(s); language;
what one says; horse
돌리다 = to spin (something);
to turn something around

말을 돌리다
[ma-reul dol-li-da]

LITERAL TRANSLATION:
to turn the words around

ACTUAL USAGE:
to change the topic of a conversation

This expression is most often used when someone deliberately changes the subject to avoid talking about a certain topic. It can also be used when someone is just beating around the bush without getting to the point right away.

A: 왜 이렇게 늦었어.

　　B: 오는데 차가 너무 막혔어.

A: 그럼 일찍 나와야지.

　　B: 우리 오늘 뭐 할까?

A: 말 돌리지 말고.

A: Why are you so late?

　　B: The traffic was so bad on my way here.

A: Then you should've left early.

　　B: What shall we do today?

A: Don't change the topic.

A: 내일 에버랜드 가자.

　　B: 에버랜드는 왜?

A: 놀이동산 계속 가고 싶었어.

　　B: 그래? 근데 너 점심 먹었어?

A: 말 돌리지 말고. 내일 갈 거야 안 갈 거야?

A: Let's go to Everland tomorrow.

　　B: Why Everland?

A: I've been wanting to go to an amusement park.

　　B: You have? By the way, did you have lunch?

A: Don't change the topic. Are we going there tomorrow or not?

CHAPTER. 11

병 = disease
주다 = to give
약 = medicine

병 주고 약 주다
[byeong ju-go yak ju-da]

ACTUAL USAGE:
to say something hurtful to someone
and then say something nice to cover it up

Saying something without thinking almost always causes a problem, whether it is making something worse or hurting someone's feelings. Often times, people try to fix the problem or cover up the damage. If a person causes a problem and tries to fix it, but the damage has already been done, you could say "병 주고 약 줘요?" to that person. This expression can also be used if a person says something hurtful, then quickly tries to come up with something to cover up his/her thoughtlessness; however, it is already too late. The offended person can then reply with "병 주고 약 주지 마세요."

A: 머리 파마했어요?

   B: 네. 어때요?

A: 파마하기 전이 더 예쁜 것 같아요. 옷도 샀어요? 이 옷 정말 잘 어울려요.

   B: 됐어요. 지금 병 주고 약 주는 거예요?

A: Did you get a perm?

   B: Yeah. How is it?

A: I think you looked prettier before the perm. Did you also get new clothes? This suits you really well.

   B: Forget it. Are you trying to comfort me after you hurt my feelings?

A: 너 남자 친구랑 헤어졌다며? 너 클럽 자주 갈 때부터 이럴 줄 알았어.

   B: 지금 놀리는 거야? 사귈 때는 몰랐는데 헤어지니까 정말 힘들다. 너무 슬퍼.

A: 힘내. 다시 좋은 사람 만날 수 있을 거야.

   B: 병 주고 약 주는 거야?

A: I heard you broke up with your boyfriend. I knew this would happen ever since you started frequently going to clubs.

   B: Are you making fun of me now? I didn't know when I was dating, but now that I broke up with him, it's so tough. I'm so sad.

A: Cheer up. You'll be able to meet someone nice again.

   B: Are you trying to comfort me after you hurt my feelings?

CHAPTER. 12

가방 = bag
끈 = string; cord; lace; strap
짧다 = to be short

가방끈이 짧다
[ga-bang-kkeu-ni jjal-tta]

LITERAL TRANSLATION:
the strap of a bag is short

ACTUAL USAGE:
to not have higher education (higher education here
usually refers to university or higher)

This idiom is normally used to describe someone who graduated from elementary school, middle/junior high school, or high school, but did not continue on to the university level. Therefore, the proverbial "bag strap" is short in comparison to someone who graduated from a university. This expression originates from the fact that the first letter of the word "background," as in "educational background," which is written as 백 or 빽 in Hangeul, has pronunciation similar to "bag" to Korean speakers' ears.

A: 우리 팀은 모두 대학원을 나왔어요.

B: 진짜요? 제가 가방끈이 제일 짧네요.

A: 그래도 실력은 제일 좋잖아요.

A: Everybody in our team graduated from graduate school.

B: Really? I have the least amount of educational background.

A: But you have the best skills.

A: 세상 살기 힘들다.

B: 왜 그래요? 취업 안 돼서 그래요?

A: 네. 가방끈이 짧은 사람은 취업도 힘들어요.

B: 힘내세요. 곧 취업 될 거예요.

A: Life is hard.

B: What's the matter? Is it because you can't get a job?

A: Yeah. If you don't have a good educational background, it's hard to get a job.

B: Cheer up. You will get a job soon.

CHAPTER. 13

머리 = head; hair
식히다 = to cool something down

머리를 식히다
[meo-ri-reul si-ki-da]

LITERAL TRANSLATION:
to cool down one's head

ACTUAL USAGE:
to get some fresh air or to relax when you have a lot of
things to do and/or when you are stressed

After thinking, working, or studying too hard and becoming really stressed out, a person needs to stop and relax. That's where 머리를 식히다 comes in. Be careful when writing this expression, as the verbs 식히다 and 시키다 are homonyms—same pronunciation, but spelled differently.

A: 어디 갔다 왔나 봐요?

    B: 네. 머리 좀 식히러 부산에 내려갔다 왔어요.

A: 좀 나아졌어요?

    B: 네. 기분이 한결 낫네요.

A: I'm guessing that you've been somewhere?

    B: Yeah. I went to Busan to get some fresh air.

A: Feel better now?

    B: Yeah, I feel much better.

A: 아까 공부한다고 못 나온다고 하더니 게임하고 있는 거예요?

    B: 10분 전까지 계속 공부하다가 잠깐 머리 식히려고 하는 거예요.

A: 책도 없잖아요!

A: You said earlier that you couldn't go out because you had to study, but you were just playing video games?

    B: I was studying until 10 minutes ago, and I'm just taking a short break now to get some fresh air.

A: You don't even have a book here!

머리를 식히다

CHAPTER. 14

눈 = eye
밟히다 = to get stepped on by something

눈에 밟히다
[nu-ne bal-pi-da]

LITERAL TRANSLATION:
to get stepped on by an eye

ACTUAL USAGE:
to miss someone and think about a person who is
physically away from you

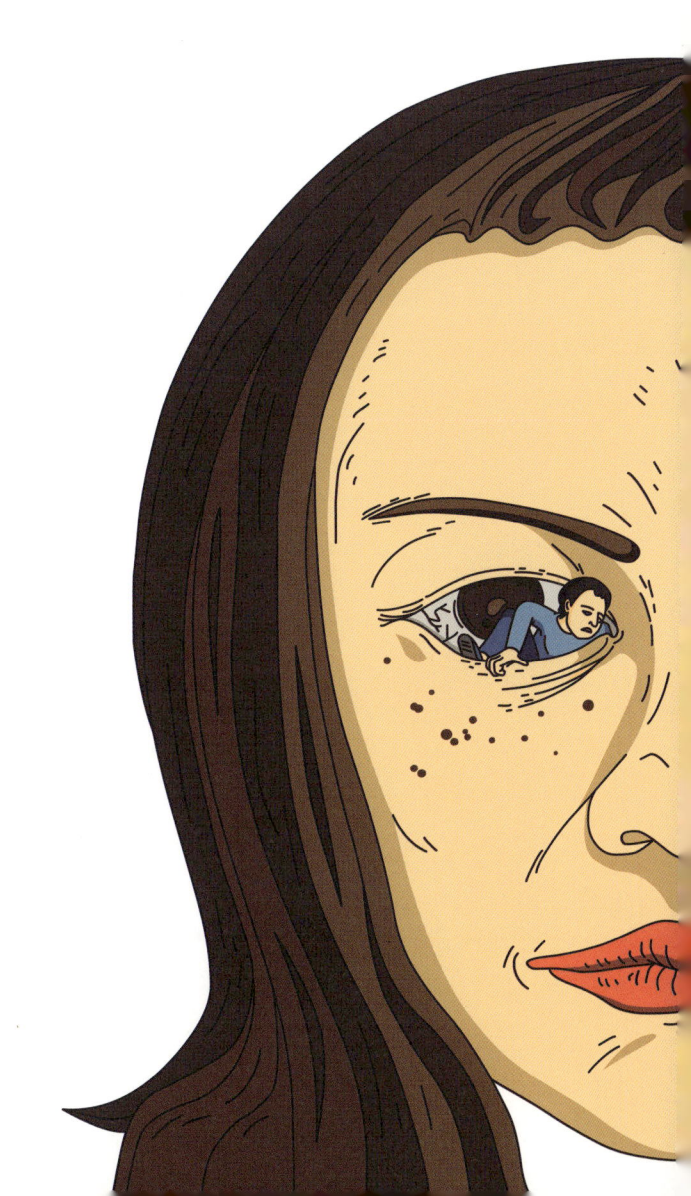

When missing or worrying about someone who is not around, people tend to think about that person every moment of the day and can't get him/her off their mind. For example, a mother who just found out that her child who lives aboard is sick can say **"아이가 눈에 밟혀요."**

A: 무슨 걱정 있어요?

 B: 어제 집 앞에서 길 잃은 강아지를 봤는데 자꾸 눈에 밟히네요.

A: 강아지요? 주인이 잘 찾아갔을 거예요. 걱정 마세요.

A: Are you worried about something?

 B: I saw a lost puppy in front of my house yesterday and I can't get it out of my head.

A: A puppy? I'm sure its owner found it and brought it back home. Don't worry.

A: 오늘 소율 씨 어디 아파요?

 B: 몰라요. 왜요?

A: 표정이 안 좋아서요. 자꾸 눈에 밟히네요.

A: Is Soyul sick today?

 B: I don't know. Why?

A: Because she doesn't look well. I can't get her out of my mind.

CHAPTER. 15

잠수 = submergence;
the act of going under water
타다 = to ride; to get on (a vehicle);
to take (a bus/subway/taxi)

잠수를 타다

[jam-su-reul ta-da]

LITERAL TRANSLATION:
to go under water

ACTUAL USAGE:
to fall off the grid/map;
to go completely out of reach;
to not answer phone calls or texts

잠수를 타다 expresses, literally, that if something is under water, especially in the deep end of the pool or a lake, it is hard to reach from the surface. If someone is unreachable by telephone, text, or e-mails for several days, they are "잠수를 타다." A similar expression in English is "to fall off the map" or "to be off the grid."

A: 은영 씨는 잠수 타는 게 취미인가 봐요.

    B: 왜요? 또 연락이 안 돼요?

A: 네. 지난주부터 전화도 안 받고, 문자도 답이 없네요.

    B: 급한 일이면 집으로 찾아가 보세요.

A: Eun-yeong seems to enjoy disappearing off the grid.

    B: Why? You can't reach her again?

A: Yeah. She hasn't been answering phone calls or text messages since last week.

    B: If it's something urgent, try visiting her at her house.

A: 요즘 현우 씨 본 적 있어요?

    B: 아니요. 그러고 보니 요즘 현우 씨가 안 보이네요.

A: 제가 한 달 전에 현우 씨한테 오만원을 빌려줬는데 갚지도 않고 잠수를 탔어요. 연락을 해도 핸드폰이 꺼져 있어요.

A: Have you seen Hyunwoo recently?

    B: No. Now that you mention it, I haven't seen him these days.

A: I lent Hyunwoo 50,000 won a month ago and he just disappeared without paying me back. When I call, his phone is turned off.

CHAPTER. 16

추위 = cold (noun)
타다 = to ride; to get on (a vehicle);
to take (a bus/subway/taxi)

추위를 타다
[chu-wi-reul ta-da]

LITERAL TRANSLATION:
to ride the cold

ACTUAL USAGE:
to be sensitive to cold (temperatures)

If translated literally, "추위를 타다" means "to ride the cold" or "to get on the cold." However, idiomatically it means "to be sensitive to the cold" or "to feel the cold temperature more easily than others." This expression can be altered to be used in regards to hot weather—더위를 타다.

A: 저는 겨울이 너무 싫어요.

B: 왜요? 저는 겨울이 제일 좋아요.

A: 제가 추위를 많이 타거든요. 추운 거 너무 싫어요.

A: I really hate the winter.

B: Why? I like the winter the most.

A: I'm very sensitive to cold. I really hate cold weather.

A: 오늘 너무 추워요.

B: 오늘요? 오늘은 안 추운데...

A: 진짜요? 전 이렇게 두껍게 입어도 추운데요?

B: 추위를 많이 타시네요.

A: It's so cold today.

B: Today? It's not cold today...

A: Really? Even though I'm wearing all these clothes, I am still cold.

B: You are very sensitive to cold.

CHAPTER. 17

54

기 = one's energy, confidence, or spirit
막히다 = to get stuck;
to be clogged; to be blocked

기가 막히다

[gi-ga ma-ki-da]

LITERAL TRANSLATION:
one's energy gets stuck or blocked

ACTUAL USAGE:
to be at a loss for words
when one hears something unbelievable

When you are "**기가 막히다**," it means that you are taken aback by something or you are at a loss for words and find something totally unbelievable. While typically used in a negative situation to express disbelief or astonishment about something, **기가 막히다** can also be used when followed by a positive adjective or verb, such as in "**기가 막히게 맛있어요**," which implies that something is so delicious that you could die.

A: 내가 기가 막혀서...

　　B: 왜? 무슨 일 있어?

A: 택배가 왔는데 물건이 깨져 있는 거야.

　　B: 정말? 그래서?

A: 반품한다니까 반품도 안 되고 환불도 안 된다고 하네.

A: I'm at a loss for words.

　　B: Why? What's wrong?

A: I received a package and the item was broken.

　　B: Really? So?

A: I told them I wanted to return it, and they said I can't return it, and I can't get a refund either.

A: 이번에 새로 나온 핸드폰 봤어요?

　　B: 아니요. 아직 못 봤어요. 어때요?

A: 정말 기가 막히게 멋져요.

　　B: 살 거예요?

A: 고민 중이에요.

A: Did you see the new cellphone that came out?

　　B: No. I haven't seen it. How is it?

A: It's amazing.

　　B: Are you going to buy it?

A: I'm thinking about it.

CHAPTER. 18

모범 = (good) example; role model
학생 = student
생 is a shortened form of 학생.

모범생

[mo-beom-saeng]

LITERAL TRANSLATION:

exemplary student

ACTUAL USAGE:

good student, model student

A "모범생" is a good example of what every student should be: always completes his/her homework, never arrives late to class, participates every day, and does well on exams. It is a combination of two words: 모범, which means a "good behavior" or "case example," and 학생, a "student."

A: 상미 씨는 학교 다닐 때 학교 안 가고 놀러 간 적 있어요?
　　B: 저요? 아니요. 학교를 어떻게 안 가요.
A: 진짜요? 상미 씨 모범생이었어요?
　　B: 네. 그렇게 안 보여요?

A: Sang-mi, have you ever skipped school and gone somewhere to play when you were attending school?
*　　B: Me? No. How can you not go to school?*
A: Really? Were you a model student?
*　　B: Yes. Do I not look like that?*

A: 소영아, 우리 오늘 학교 가지 말고 영화 보러 갈까?
　　B: 영화? 안 돼. 오늘 수업 중요해.
A: 아휴... 모범생처럼 그러지 말고 영화 보러 가자.
　　B: 안 되는데... 딱 한 번만이야.

A: Soyeong, shall we skip school and go see a movie today?
*　　B: Movie? No, I can't. Today's class is important.*
A: (Sigh) Don't act like a model student and let's go see a movie.
*　　B: No, I really shouldn't... (Okay,) it's only this once, then.*

CHAPTER. 19

반 = half

반반
[ban-ban]

LITERAL TRANSLATION:
half and half

ACTUAL USAGE:
half and half

반반 is a repetition of the word "반," which means "half." It is commonly used when ordering food. For example, when ordering fried chicken in Korea, some people often have a hard time deciding what they would like to order, plain fried chicken or fried chicken with sauce. Therefore, they often end up ordering both. In this case, they can say that they would like "반반." This expression also applies to various other situations. 반반 can be used when paying in a restaurant and you would like to split the bill. Another situation you can use 반반 is while expressing opinions; you could be half agreeing and half disagreeing with something. Also note that, in Korean, there are many words that are basically a repetition of the same word, such as "빨리빨리" which means "quick quick," or "반짝반짝" which translates to "twinkle twinkle."

A: 오늘 저녁은 치킨 어때?
　　B: 좋아! 양념치킨? 후라이드?
A: 반반!

A: How about having fried chicken for dinner tonight?
　　B: Good! Sweet and sour fried chicken? Plain fried chicken?
A: Half and half!

A: 난 포테이토 피자 먹고 싶은데 언니가 싫대.
　　B: 언니는 뭐 먹고 싶다고 하는데?
A: 치즈 피자.
　　B: 그럼 반반 시켜.

A: I want to eat potato pizza, but my older sister doesn't want it.
　　B: What does she say she wants to eat?
A: Cheese pizza.
　　B: Then order half and half.

CHAPTER. 20

잘 = well
나가다 = to attend; to get out;
to go forward

잘나가다
[jal-la-ga-da]

LITERAL TRANSLATION:
something moves forward well

ACTUAL USAGE:
to be popular;
to be successful

The literal translation of "잘나가다" is "to move forward well." As an idiomatic expression, you can use this about a person or a product. Whether a person or a product, if they 잘나가다, it means the person or product is popular. If 잘나가다 is used to describe a product, it means many people look for it and buy it. If it's used about a person, it means that the person is sought-after by many people and/or that person is successful.

A: 수영이 기억나? 고등학교 동창.

   B: 수영이? 키 크고 안경 쓴 애?

A: 맞아, 맞아. 학교 다닐 때 별로였는데 요즘 진짜 잘나간대.

A: Do you remember Suyeong? Our classmate from high school.

   B: Suyeong? The tall one with glasses?

A: Yeah, yeah. He wasn't popular back when we were in school, but I hear that he's really popular these days.

A: 어제 클럽을 갔는데 3명이 내 전화번호 달라고 했어.

   B: 잘난 척하는 거야?

A: 잘난 척은 무슨. 당연한 거지. 역시 난 잘나간단 말야.

A: I went to a club yesterday and three people asked for my phone number.

   B: Are you showing off?

A: No, I'm not showing off. It's a natural thing to happen. I'm so popular, as always!

CHAPTER. 21

마음 = mind; heart
굴뚝 = chimney

마음은 굴뚝 같다

[ma-eu-meun gul-ttuk gat-tta]

ACTUAL USAGE:

I really want to do it (but I can't).

No one really knows the exact origin of this expression, but one widely believed hypothesis is that 마음은 굴뚝 같다 stems from back in the old days when Korean homes had a chimney to exhaust the smoke from burning wood used to heat the floors or cook. Wood costs money, so poorer people eagerly worked and hoped that they could always have smoke coming out of their chimney, especially during the long winter months. For example, if your friend asks you to help her with something, but you are either too busy or not interested in helping her, "마음은 굴뚝 같아요." Sometimes this expression is used as an excuse to get out of doing something without being rude, "마음은 굴뚝 같지만 너무 바빠요."

A: 이번 토요일에 제 생일 파티 할 거예요. 선영 씨도 꼭 오세요.

B: 토요일에요? 저는 회사에 일이 있어서 못 갈 것 같아요.

A: 정말요? 너무 아쉬워요.

B: 저도 가고 싶은 마음은 굴뚝 같아요.

A: This Saturday, I am having my birthday party. Seonyeog, be sure to come.

B: Saturday? I have work to do at my company, so I won't be able to go.

A: Really? That's too bad.

B: I would really love to be there, too. (But I can't.)

A: 터키 가고 싶다.

B: 그러면 가면 되지.

A: 마음은 굴뚝 같지. 돈이 없어서 그렇지.

A: I want to go to Turkey.

B: Then you should go there.

A: I'd love to go right now. I just don't have the money.

CHAPTER. 22

오리발 = duck's feet; flippers
내밀다 = to stick out; to stretch out

오리발 내밀다
[o-ri-bal nae-mil-da]

The full expression is "닭 잡아먹고 오리발 내밀다" ("to eat a chicken and stick out a duck's foot"), and the shortened version is "오리발 내밀다." As an idiomatic expression, it is used when you want to hide the truth about something that you did. When you are sure that a person did something and this person is denying that he/she did it, you can say, "오리발 내밀지 마," which can be translated to "don't lie to me."

A: 이거 니가 고장 냈지?

    B: 아니야. 나... 난... 난 아니야.

A: 오리발 내밀지 말고 빨리 말해.

    B: 미안해... 일부러 그런 건 아니고...

A: You broke this, right?

    B: No... It's not...not me...

A: Don't deny it and just tell me quickly.

    B: I'm sorry. I didn't do it on purpose.

A: 차가 왜 이래요?

    B: 주차장에 세워 놨는데 이렇게 됐어요.

A: 누가 그랬는지 알아요?

    B: 아무래도 옆집 사람인 것 같은데 아니라고 오리발 내밀고 있어요.

A: What happened to your car?

    B: I parked it in the parking lot and this happened.

A: Do you know who did that?

    B: I'm pretty sure it's my neighbor, but he's denying it and saying he didn't do it.

CHAPTER. 23

김칫국 = kimchi soup
마시다 = to drink

김칫국부터 마시다

[gim-chit-guk-bu-teo ma-si-da]

LITERAL TRANSLATION:

to drink kimchi soup first

ACTUAL USAGE:

to be excited over something
that you don't know for sure will happen
and/or plan out things first

김칫국부터 마시다 comes from the full expression, "떡 줄 사람은 생각도 않는데, 김칫국부터 마신다," which roughly translates to "the person who might give you rice cakes is not even thinking about (giving you the cakes), but you drink your kimchi soup first." 떡 is a delicious treat, and in the past, it was common to eat 떡 (rice cakes) with cold kimchi soup because the 떡 is too dry without some sort of soup or water. If you are excited about getting some 떡 and you drink the kimchi soup out of excitement before eating the 떡, should you ever get any, you may struggle with eating the dry rice cakes when you get them. The same goes for making plans about something that has not happened yet or if someone is unsure about something happening, but yet, he/she is still making plans out of excitement. Some English equivalent are "don't count your chickens before they hatch" and "don't jump the gun."

A: 오늘 승진 결과 나오는 거 알아요?

  B: 진짜요? 경화 씨는 승진할 거니까 좋겠어요.

A: 아니에요. 미리 김칫국부터 마시고 싶지 않아요.

A: Do you know that the promotion results are coming out today?

  B: Really? Kyung-hwa, you will get promoted so you must be happy.

A: No. I don't want to be excited about something that hasn't happened.

A: 뭐 하고 있어요?

  B: 연말 보너스 나오면 여행 가려고 알아보고 있어요.

A: 김칫국부터 마시지 말아요. 연말 보너스 안 나올 수도 있대요.

A: What are you doing?

  B: I'm looking for some information so that I can go on a trip when I get my year-end bonus.

A: Don't be excited too early. I heard that we might not get the year-end bonus.

CHAPTER. 24

허리가 휘다
[heo-ri-ga hwi-da]

LITERAL TRANSLATION:

One's waist is bent.

ACTUAL USAGE:

One's financial burden is too heavy.

This idiomatic expression is usually used when speaking of financial burdens, but more specifically about parents having to work hard to support their children. This expression originates from the fact that many parents used to do physical labor to support the family in the past, and from doing too much labor, they can develop a chronic backache or a back that is not straight.

A: 무슨 애가 이렇게 많이 먹어?

B: 먹는 거 갖고 왜 그래! 치사하게.

A: 치사하긴. 너 먹이느라 내 허리가 휜다.

A: You eat so much for a kid!

B: Come on, don't be so cheap with food.

A: I'm not being cheap. I have to work my tail off to feed you.

A: 요즘 사교육 열풍이 장난 아니래요.

B: 맞아요. 학교 끝나고 학원을 몇 개나 다니는 애들이 많다고 하네요.

A: 아휴... 부모들 허리만 휘겠어요.

A: I heard that private education craze is no joke these days.

B: Yeah. I heard many children go to a bunch of private institutes after school.

A: (Sigh) The parents will have to work really hard to pay for it.

CHAPTER. 25

김 = steam
새다 = to leak

김새다

[gim-sae-da]

LITERAL TRANSLATION:

The steam leaks.

ACTUAL USAGE:

One's fun is spoiled.;
One's enthusiasm dies down.

To understand this expressions, we need to take a closer look at the literal translation. Imagine you are cooking rice with a rice cooker and you open it too early. All the steam is released and your rice is undercooked and not ready. Undercooked rice is a negative result and, idiomatically, 김새다 also has a negative connotation, meaning that one's fun is spoiled or one's enthusiasm dies down. If you have the idea to plan a surprise party for someone, for example, but this person finds out about it beforehand, then your excitement dies down and you feel disappointed. You do not want to continue planning the surprise any longer because there is no point in doing so anymore. Thus, you could imagine the 김 or the "steam" to be your excitement or interest, and when combined with 새다, it means "to lose your excitement" or "to lose your interest." You could then say: "아 김샜어," meaning "ah, I'm disappointed... I don't want to do this anymore."

A: 오늘 초대 손님 누구 오는 줄 알아요?
　　B: 아니요. 진짜 궁금해요.
A: 유명한 사람은 아니래요.
　　B: 에이, 김샜네. 기대하고 있었는데...

A: Do you know who the invited guests for today are?
　　B: No. I'm really curious.
A: I heard they are not famous.
　　B: Oh, that spoils the fun. I was looking forward to it.

A: 아... 김샜다.
　　B: 왜요?
A: 이 영화 보려고 기대하고 있었는데 친구가 내용을 다 말해버렸어요.

A: That spoiled the fun.
　　B: Why?
A: I was going to watch this movie, and I was looking forward to it, but my friend told me the whole storyline.

CHAPTER. 26

매운맛을 보여 주다
[mae-un ma-seul bo-yeo-ju-da]

LITERAL TRANSLATION:
to show someone the spicy taste of something

ACTUAL USAGE:
to show someone how angry you are by, usually, being physically violent; to show someone who doesn't believe in how capable you are of something

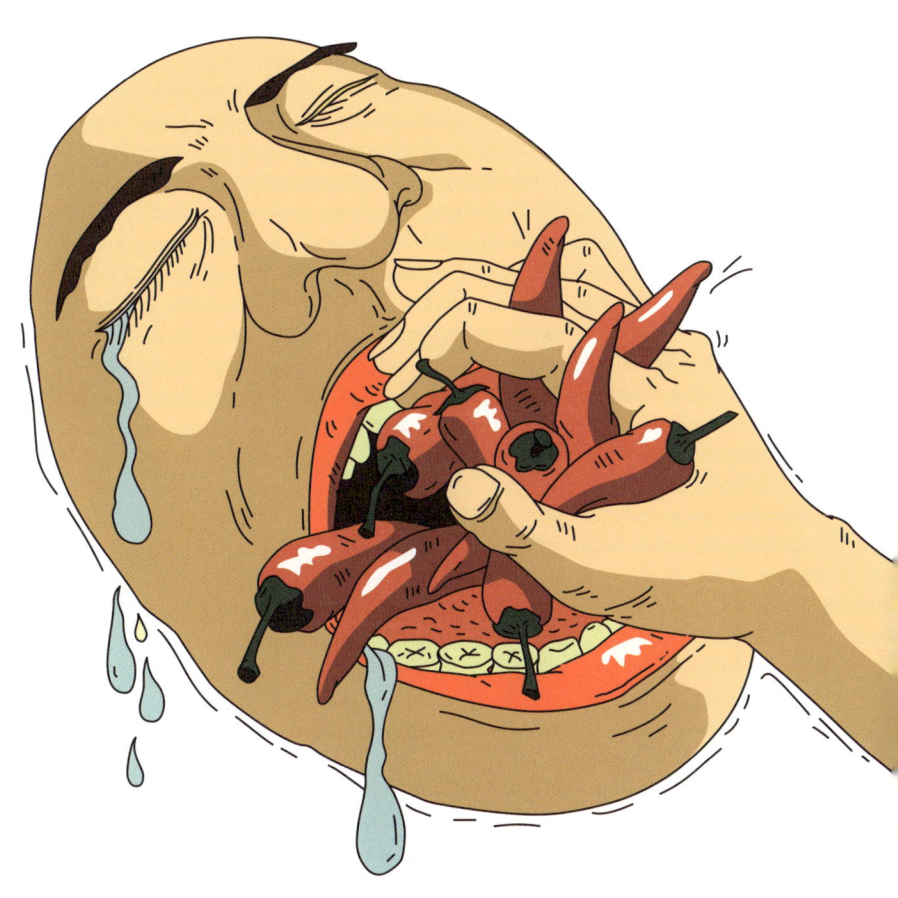

You are angry and you want to express this anger by being violent or threatening someone, in which you can say "매운맛을 보여줄 거야!" or "I will show you how angry I am!" However, 매운맛을 보여 주다 can also have a slightly different meaning. For instance, in a situation where no one believes in you and your abilities, you could feel offended and react by thinking to yourself, "매운맛을 보여줄 거야," which translate to, "wait and see, I will show you what I'm capable of" or "I will show you how it's done!" In this situation, you want to prove something to someone; you want to prove them wrong. You're feeling ignored or disregarded and are frustrated because of it.

A: 요즘 매일 운동해?

B: 응. 다음 주에 운동회가 있거든. 이번에 잘해서 매운맛을 보여줄 거야.

A: 우와. 화이팅!

A: Do you exercise everyday these days?

B: Yeah. We have field day next week. I'm going to do well this time and show the other team what we've got.

A: Wow. Good luck!

A: 중간고사 또 2등 했어.

B: 2등? 우와. 진짜 잘했다.

A: 아니야. 내가 1등을 해야 하는데, 수진이가 또 1등이잖아. 지금부터 열심히 해서 다음 시험에서는 수진이한테 매운맛을 보여줄 거야.

A: I came in second place in the mid-term exams again.

B: second place? Wow. Well done!

A: No, I have to get first place. Sujin took first place again. I'm going to study hard from now and show Sujin what I've got in the next exams.

CHAPTER. 27

물 = water
만나다 = to meet (up)
고기 = meat; fish

물 만난 고기

[mul man-nan go-gi]

LITERAL TRANSLATION:
fish that met water

ACTUAL USAGE:
to feel comfortable about doing something;
to be very good at something in a certain situation

Literally this expression means "a fish that met water." In English there's the expression "fish out of water," which means you are feeling uncomfortable in a certain situation, or you are out of your familiar surroundings. With this Korean expression however, the opposite is true. We know that fish are most comfortable in the water. When you're good at something, you feel very comfortable doing it and people can say that you are a 물 만난 고기. In English you could translate this to "being in your element" or being good at what you're doing "like a fish in the water," It's usually a sudden occurrence as in entering a certain field and suddenly feeling completely comfortable in it. For example, you might not have known that you were born to be a broadcaster but then you try it out and feel completely at ease. You're in your element. If you've been doing something for a very long time and are good at it for that reason you usually don't use this expression.

A: 어제 회식하고 나서 클럽에 갔었어요.

B: 진짜요? 재미있었어요?

A: 네. 얌전한 줄 알았던 미영 씨가 물 만난 고기처럼 춤을 추더라고요.

A: We went to a club yesterday after the company dinner.

B: Really? Did you have fun?

A: Yeah. I thought Miyeong was quiet and shy, but she was dancing there very comfortably and happily.

A: 어제 체육대회 잘했어요?

B: 네. 우리 팀이 이겼어요.

A: 진짜요? 수진 씨 팀에 운동 잘하는 사람들이 많았어요?

B: 그럼요. 다들 물 만난 고기 같았어요.

A: Did you do well at the sports day event yesterday?

B: Yes, my team won.

A: Really? Sujin, were there a lot of people who were good at sports on your team?

B: Sure! They were all very skillful, like fish swimming in the water.

CHAPTER. 28

입 = mouth
짧다 = to be short

입이 짧다
[i-bi jjal-tta]

LITERAL TRANSLATION:
to have a short mouth

ACTUAL USAGE:
to eat only a small amount of food;
to have a small appetite

Although the literal translation of "입이 짧다" is "to have a short mouth," you cannot literally have a "short mouth." 입이 짧다 means that someone has a small appetite. In English, you could say that someone "eats like a bird." If someone can never finish his/her meals and only eats a tiny amount each time, they are an "입이 짧은 사람," a person with a small appetite. In some cases, it can also refer to picky eaters, since when someone is picky about food, he/she tends to not each much. You only choose the things you like, which is often the case with children; therefore many children can be 입이 짧은 children.

A: 애들이 왜 이렇게 말랐어요?

    B: 애들이 입이 너무 짧아서 잘 안 먹어요.

A: 걱정되시겠어요.

A: Why are the kids so skinny?

    B: They have a small appetite, so they don't eat much.

A: You must be worried.

A: 우리 가족들은 입이 짧아서 치킨 한 마리를 다 못 먹어.

    B: 진짜? 우리는 두 마리 시켜도 부족한데. 부럽다.

A: 우리 가족은 항상 남아.

A: My family has a small appetite so we can't even finish one fried chicken.

    B: Really? For my family, even if we order two fried chickens, it's not enough. I'm jealous.

A: We always have leftovers.

CHAPTER. 29

발목 = ankle
잡다 = to grab; to catch; to hold

발목 잡다
[bal-mok jap-tta]

LITERAL TRANSLATION:
to grab someone's ankle

ACTUAL USAGE:
something prevents someone
from doing something

Literally translated, this would mean you are grabbing someone's ankle. Idiomatically, however, it is used when someone or something is holding you down, or preventing you from doing what you want to do. You can use this about anything that prevents you from doing something you hope to do, including time. An example of this expression is if you were working toward your dream as a succesful sports player, but you got a bad injury(**부상**), you can say, "**부상이 발목을 잡았어요.**"

1

A: 저는 부장님 사무실에 오기 전에 퇴근할게요.

　　B: 부장님한테 인사 안 하고 가려고요?

A: 부장님 오시면 발목 잡혀요. 분명히 술 마시자고 하실 거예요.

A: I'll leave the office before the manager comes back.

　　B: You want to go without saying bye to him?

A: If he gets here, I will be stuck. I'm sure he will ask me to drink with him.

2

A: 이 회사에 근무한 지 얼마나 됐지?

　　B: 3년 차입니다.

A: 근데 아직도 일을 이렇게 처리해?

　　B: 죄송합니다.

A: 너 때문에 내가 진급을 못 하고 있어. 내 발목 좀 그만 잡아라.

A: How long have you worked at this company?

　　B: It's been three years.

A: And you still handle work so poorly?

　　B: I'm sorry.

A: I can't get promoted because of you. Please stop dragging me down.

CHAPTER. 30

사랑 = love
식다 = something becomes cold

사랑이 식다
[sa-rang-i sik-tta]

LITERAL TRANSLATION:

Love becomes cold.

ACTUAL USAGE:

The love for someone/something is fading.

사랑이 식다 is used when the love for someone or something is fading, such as when you fall in love with someone, the love for that person at the beginning is very strong. As time passes by, however, you can change the view you have on that person and your love sometimes isn't the same anymore. It can also be used for an object that you cherish.

A: 남자 친구가 요즘 연락이 뜸해요.
　　　B: 진짜요? 요즘 일이 바쁜 거 아닐까요?
A: 아니에요. 사랑이 식은 것 같아요.

A: My boyfriend seldom contacts me these days.
　　　B: Really? Maybe it's because his work is busy?
A: No. I think he doesn't love me as much anymore.

A: 요즘 여자 친구랑 잘 지내?
　　　B: 그럼 아주 잘 지내지.
A: 사귄 지 얼마나 됐어?
　　　B: 세 달 정도.
A: 이제 사랑이 식을 때가 됐어.

A: Are things going well with your girlfriend these days?
　　　B: Of course. We are getting along fine.
A: How long have you been dating?
　　　B: About three months.
A: It's about time you fell out of love.

CHAPTER. 31

닭살 = chicken's meat; goosebump
커플 = couple
(In Korean, the word, 커플 usually refers to unmarried couples.)

닭살 커플
[dak-sal keo-peul]

LITERAL TRANSLATION:

goosebump couple

ACTUAL USAGE:

A couple who is not shy about doing pulic display of affection.

This expression is half Korean and half Konglish. "닭" means "chicken" or "rooster," and "살" means "flesh." Thus, "닭살" means "chicken flesh," but is often translated as "goosebumps." When you talk about the actual skin of a chicken, people usually call it "(닭) 껍질," not "닭살." "커플" refers to the English word "couple," married or unmarried. Therefore, as an idiomatic expression, a 닭살 커플 is a couple that is not shy about publicly displaying their affection for one another which gives others goosebumps, either in a bad way or in a good and "cute" way. For example, a couple who keeps on feeding each other at the restaurant can be considered a 닭살 커플.

A: 현정 씨랑 진호 씨랑 사귀는 줄 몰랐어요.
    B: 진짜요? 둘이 닭살 커플로 유명해요.
A: 정말요? 저는 상상이 안 되네요.

A: I didn't know Hyeonjeong and Jinho were dating.
    B: Really? They are famous for being such love birds.
A: Really? I can't imagine.

A: 남자 친구는 잘해줘?
    B: 응. 너무 잘해 줘. 요즘 정말 행복해.
A: 신기하다. 니가 이렇게 닭살 커플이 될 줄이야.

A: Is your boyfriend nice to you?
    B: Yes. He's so nice to me. I'm so happy these days.
A: That's amazing. I had no idea that you would become such love birds.

CHAPTER. 32

눈 = eye
붙이다 = to stick/glue things together;
to attach

눈을 붙이다

[nu-neul bu-chi-da]

LITERAL TRANSLATION:
to stick one's eyes together

ACTUAL USAGE:
to get some shut-eye

This expression is used when someone rests, but not for a long time. For example, when you are at the office and you want to rest, it can be rude to just say "잘게요" ("I'm going to sleep"). It is more accepted if you say "눈 좀 붙일게요." In English, it can be translated as "to get some shut-eye."

A: 보람 씨 오늘 정말 피곤해 보여요.
　　B: 어제 일이 있어서 잠을 못 잤어요.
A: 잠깐 눈 좀 붙이세요.
　　B: 네. 고마워요.

A: Boram, you look really tired today.
　　B: Something came up yesterday and I couldn't sleep.
A: Get some sleep for a while.
　　B: Yeah. Thank you.

A: 어제 야근했어요?
　　B: 사실 어제 집에 못 들어갔어요.
A: 일이 그렇게 많았어요?
　　B: 네. 너무 피곤해요. 저 잠깐만 눈 좀 붙이고 올게요.

A: Did you do overtime work yesterday?
　　B: In fact, I couldn't get home yesterday.
A: You had that much work yesterday?
　　B: Yes. I'm so tired. I'll go take a nap for a little while and come back.

CHAPTER. 33

'밀'다 = to push
'당'기다 = to pull

밀당
[mil-ttang]

LITERAL TRANSLATION:
to push and pull

ACTUAL USAGE:
to play hard to get and then
to be sweet to the same person

This expression is a combination of the verbs 밀다 and 당기다 and is used to describe a certain situation that is happening in a romantic relationship. Usually, 밀당 is an action done by girls and it means that one moment the girl is acting as though she is interested, and the next she isn't and becomes distant. It usually happens in the beginning of a relationship when one doesn't want to appear easy to get. It is sort of a game that couples play, and just as the verbs 밀다 and 당기다 suggest, both parties in the relationship are pushing and pulling away at the same time. In English, this is known as "playing hard to get" and is a way to test your relationship partner to see if he/she is serious or not.

A: 주말에 소개팅했는데 이 남자 좀 이상해요.

B: 왜요? 연락 아직 없어요?

A: 문자만 왔어요. 전화는 없고요.

B: 혹시 그 남자 밀당하고 있는 거 아니에요?

A: I went on a blind date last weekend, and the guy is a little strange.

B: Why? He hasn't contacted you yet?

A: I've only received text messages. No phone calls.

B: Is he playing hard to get, by any chance?

A: 그 여자랑 잘 만나고 있어?

B: 잘 만나고 있어.

A: 그럼 사귀는 거야?

B: 벌써 사귀면 안 되지. 연애는 밀당이 중요해!

A: Is everything going well with that girl?

B: Everything is going alright.

A: Then are you guys a couple?

B: We can't be a couple yet. In dating, playing hard to get is important.

CHAPTER. 34

벼락 = thunderbolt; lightning
벼락이 치다 = lightening strikes

벼락치기
[**byeo-rak-chi-gi**]

LITERAL TRANSLATION:

the striking of lightning

ACTUAL USAGE:

cramming (before a test)

"벼락치기" literally translates to "the striking of lightning." Idiomatically, it refers to a person who studies last-minute the night before an exam because he or she hasn't continuously been studying. That person needs to quickly catch up on everything right now in order to pass. One can also say this person is "cramming" for an exam. It usually isn't a good idea to do 벼락치기 before an exam, and often the knowledge you obtain by 벼락치기 doesn't stick with you in the long term.

A: 시험공부 안 해? 다음 주에 시험이잖아.
　　B: 시험 공부를 벌써부터 해? 그럴 필요 없어.
A: 너 또 벼락치기 하려고?
　　B: 당연하지.

A: Are you not studying for your exam? You have an exam next week.
　　B: Study for the exam already? There's no need to.
A: You are going to cram for the exam again?
　　B: Of course.

A: 어제 시험 다 망쳤어요.
　　B: 그럴 줄 알았어요. 벼락치기 하니까 그렇죠.
A: 제가 공부한 곳에서는 하나도 안 나왔어요.

A: I screwed up all my exams yesterday.
　　B: I knew you would. That's because you cram for your exams.
A: None of the questions were from what I studied.

CHAPTER. 35

배 = stomach; belly
아프다 = to be sick; to be ill; to hurt

배가 아프다
[bae-ga a-peu-da]

LITERAL TRANSLATION:

to have a stomachache

ACTUAL USAGE:

to be jealous (of someone who you know)

When it's used literally, 배가 아프다 means that you have a stomachache, but it can also be used when you are jealous of someone else's success or happiness. For example, imagine taking part in a competition for something with a friend, but your friend wins and you lose. In this case, you are jealous of him or her and feel a little sad and disappointed at the same time. It makes you feel "배가 아프다." An important factor of this expression is, however, that you don't use it about someone you don't know very well, such as a famous musician or actor. When someone close to you succeeds at something and you feel a pang of jealousy and can say "아, 배가 아프다" ("Ah, I'm so jealous"), all the while thinking "Why is that person so lucky? Why not me?!" When you say "배가 아프다," it also conveys the slight feeling of bad intention, because you might not think that person deserved what he or she got. A similar English idiom is "green with envy."

A: 현경 씨 사업이 정말 잘된다고 해요.
　　B: 정말 잘됐어요.
A: 그렇죠. 축하할 일인데 기분은 별로네요.
　　B: 왜요? 남 잘되니까 배 아파요?

A: I heard that Hyeonkyeong's business is doing really well.
　　B: That's great.
A: Yeah. It's something we should congratulate but I don't feel so great.
　　B: Why? Now that she's successful, you are jealous?

A: 테리스 한국어 진짜 잘한다.
　　B: 그러게. 한국어 발표에서 1등 해서 또 한국 간대.
A: 진짜? 아... 배 아프네.

A: Terris speaks Korean so well.
　　B: Yeah. He came in first place in the Korean presentation, so he's going to Korea again.
A: Really? I'm jealous.

CHAPTER. 36

잘 = well

나다 = to grow; to occur; to break out; (something) comes out

잘나다 = to be born well

- 척하다 = to pretend

잘난 척하다
[jal-lan cheo-ka-da]

LITERAL TRANSLATION:
to pretend to have been born and brought up well

ACTUAL USAGE:
to brag

잘난 척하다 is used to brag about anything and everything: yourself, skills, money, parents, siblings, etc. It is a very common expression, but since no one likes someone who brags or shows off a lot, when someone is referred to as "잘난 척하다," it's never a good thing.

A: 현정 씨, 수민 씨랑 친해요?

B: 최근에 좀 친해졌어요. 왜요?

A: 수민 씨, 잘난 척이 심한 것 같아요. 안 그래요?

B: 그래요? 전 잘 모르겠던데...

A: Hyeonjeong, are you close to Sumin?

B: I've gotten close to him recently. Why?

A: I think he's a little too arrogant and snobbish.

B: Really? I didn't really feel that way.

A: 야호! 역시 난...

B: 왜? 좋은 일 있어?

A: 한국어 발표 대회에서 1등 했어.

B: 우와. 멋지다!

A: 멋지긴. 당연한 일이지.

B: 또 잘난 척한다.

A: Woohoo! As always, I'm great!

B: Why? Something good happened?

A: I came in first place in the Korean speech contest.

B: Wow. That's cool!

A: Nah, it was expected.

B: You're bragging again.

CHAPTER. 37

사 = Sino-Korean number for four
차원 = dimension
사차원 = the fourth dimension

사차원
[**sa-cha-won**]

LITERAL TRANSLATION:
the fourth dimension

ACTUAL USAGE:
someone who thinks differently from others

사차원 is a slang expression that is often used to describe someone who is eccentric or someone who thinks differently from others. These people are often hard to predict and usually other people don't really understand them. It's hard to say it's a swear word, but it is usually associated with a negative connotation, and calling someone a 사차원 can be considered offensive.

A: 오늘 하늘 봤어요?

    B: 하늘이요? 왜요? 오늘 날씨 이상하던데...

A: 날씨가 문제가 아니에요. UFO가 하늘에 떠 있었어요.

    B: 네? 기영 씨, 정말 사차원이네요.

A: Did you see the sky today?

    B: The sky? Why? The weather was weird today.

A: The weather is not the problem. There was a UFO in the sky.

    B: What? Kiyoung, you really are bizzarre.

A: 어제 소개팅 어땠어?

    B: 소개팅? 말하기도 싫어.

A: 왜? 예쁘다고 좋아하면서 나갔잖아.

    B: 완전 사차원이더라고.

A: How did the blind date go yesterday?

    B: The blind date? I don't even want to talk about it.

A: Why? You were excited that the girl was pretty when you were leaving.

    B: She turned out to be really weird.

CHAPTER. 38

손 = hand
보다 = to see, to watch, to look

손보다

[son-bo-da]

ACTUAL USAGE:

to fix something; to be violent toward;
to have a word with someone to fix their attitude

In an idiomatic sense, 손보다 is used to express the use of the hands to accomplish something, meaning "to take care of something" or "to fix something when it is not working well." It can also be used when someone is acting rude, not being very nice, or is doing something wrong to you or someone else. You may feel the need to have a word with this person or "손보다" ("to use your hands/fists to fix his/her attitude").

A: 윤아 씨, 오늘 안 좋은 일 있어요?

B: 아... 과장님이 자꾸 이상한 말 해요.

A: 정말요? 제가 좀 손봐 줄까요?

B: 말이라도 고마워요.

A: Yoona, is there anything wrong today?

B: The manager keeps saying strange things.

A: Really? Do you want me to kick his butt?

B: It's nice of you to say that for me. Thank you.

A: 세탁기가 또 고장 난 것 같아요. 이상한 소리가 나요.

B: 또요? 그거 손본 지 얼마 안 되지 않았어요?

A: 일주일밖에 안 된 것 같은데 이러네요.

A: I think the washing machine is broken again. It makes weird sounds.

B: Again? Didn't you get it fixed not long ago?

A: I think it's only been a week now, but it's doing that.

CHAPTER. 39

앞 = front
뒤 = back
막히다 = to get stuck;
to be clogged; to be blocked

앞뒤가 막히다
[ap-dwi-ga ma-ki-da]

LITERAL TRANSLATION:
to be stuck front and back

ACTUAL USAGE:
to be very narrow-minded;
not be flexible with thoughts

앞뒤가 막히다 is an expression that describes a person who is very narrow-minded or stubborn. When someone is not very flexible with his/her thoughts, you can describe that person using this expression. This type of person usually won't take your advice, and/or rarely thinks outside of the box.

A: 수정 씨, 이 일을 왜 다시 하고 있어요?

B: 부장님이 줄 간격이 이상하다고 다시 하래요.

A: 아휴... 정말 앞뒤가 막힌 사람이에요.

A: Sujeong, why are you doing this work again?

B: The manager told me to do it again, saying that the spacing is strange.

A: (Sigh) He's so narrow-minded.

A: 사과가 너무 먹고 싶은데 편의점에서 안 팔아요.

B: 마트에 가면 되잖아요.

A: 편의점이 단골이라서요. 마트에서 물건을 사면 미안하잖아요.

B: 암튼... 앞뒤가 꽉 막혀서...

A: I really want to eat an apple, but the convenience store doesn't sell apples.

B: You can go to a grocery store.

A: I am a regular customer at the convenience store. I will feel bad if I buy stuff from the grocery store.

B: Like always, you're so narrow-minded.

CHAPTER. 40

하늘 = sky
노랗다 = to be yellow

하늘이 노랗다

[**ha-neu-ri no-ra-ta**]

LITERAL TRANSLATION:

the sky is yellow

ACTUAL USAGE:

to feel shocked or panicked
when hearing bad news

Used to describe how one feels when hearing bad news and/or when something bad happens, 하늘이 노랗다 is often used with the sentence ending —아/어/여지다, which means "to become + adjective." Used as "하늘이 노래지다," the expression describes the sky turning yellow after hearing bad or shocking news, just as the sky turns a yellow-ish color before or during a bad thunderstorm.

A: 괜찮아요? 차 사고 났었다면서요?

    B: 지금은 괜찮아요. 아까는 정말 하늘이 노랗게 보였어요.

A: 안 다쳐서 정말 다행이에요.

A: Are you okay? I heard you got into a car accident.

    B: I'm fine now. Earlier, I really felt like the sky was yellow.

A: I'm so glad that you didn't get hurt.

A: 아... 내일 시험인데 큰일이다.

    B: 왜? 공부 안 했어?

A: 응. 못 했어.

    B: 시험 내일이잖아. 어쩌려고.

A: 몰라. 하늘이 노랗다.

A: The exam day is tomorrow. I'm in trouble.

    B: Why? You didn't study?

A: No, I couldn't.

    B: The exam is tomorrow. What are you going to do?

A: I don't know. I feel hopeless.

CHAPTER. 41

붕어빵 = a bun/bread shaped like a carp (fish) and stuffed with red bean paste

붕어빵이다
[bung-eo-ppang-i-da]

LITERAL TRANSLATION:
a bun/bread shaped like a carp (fish)
and stuffed with red bean paste

ACTUAL USAGE:
two people look exactly the same

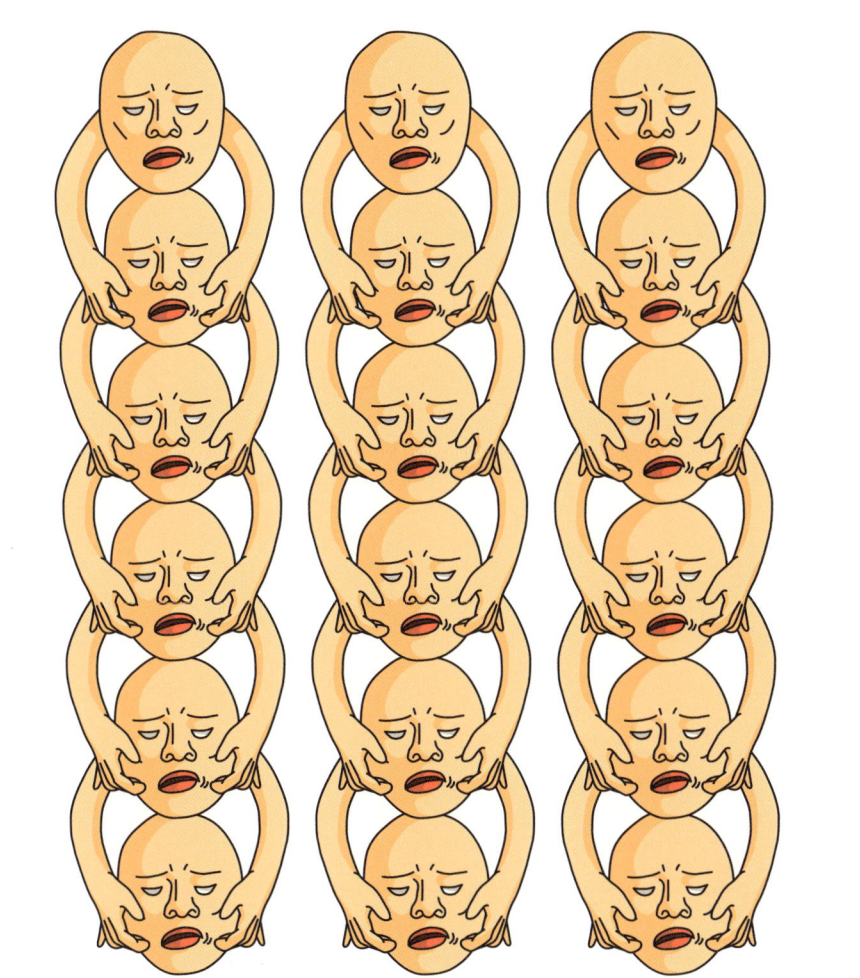

붕어빵 is a carp (fish)-shaped bun stuffed with sweet red bean paste. Often times, you will see these tasty and popular winter treats made by street vendors using a machine that has several fish-shaped molds. Each mold is identical in shape, size, and detail so the 붕어빵 will all look the same. When you describe two people, usually a parent and his/her child, as "붕어빵이다." you are implying that they resemble each other or act and talk in the same way, just as all 붕어빵 tend to look the same. A similar English expression is "chip off the old block."

A: 태은이 엄마랑 진짜 똑같이 생겼지?
   B: 진짜 엄마 닮았네. 붕어빵이다.
A: 그치? 너무 신기해.

A: Tae-eun really looks like her mom, right?
   B: She really looks like her mom. She's like a carbon copy.
A: Right? It's amazing.

A: 윤아 동생 봤어요?
   B: 아니요. 둘이 닮았어요?
A: 네. 둘이 완전 붕어빵이에요.

A: Did you see Yoona's younger sister?
   B: No. Do they look alike?
A: Yeah. They are complete carbon copies.

CHAPTER. 42

눈 = eye
넣다 = to put (something) in
아프다 = to hurt; to be sick

눈에 넣어도 아프지 않다
[nu-ne neo-eo-do a-peu-ji an-ta]

LITERAL TRANSLATION:
to not hurt even if you put it in your eyes

ACTUAL USAGE:
to love someone a lot

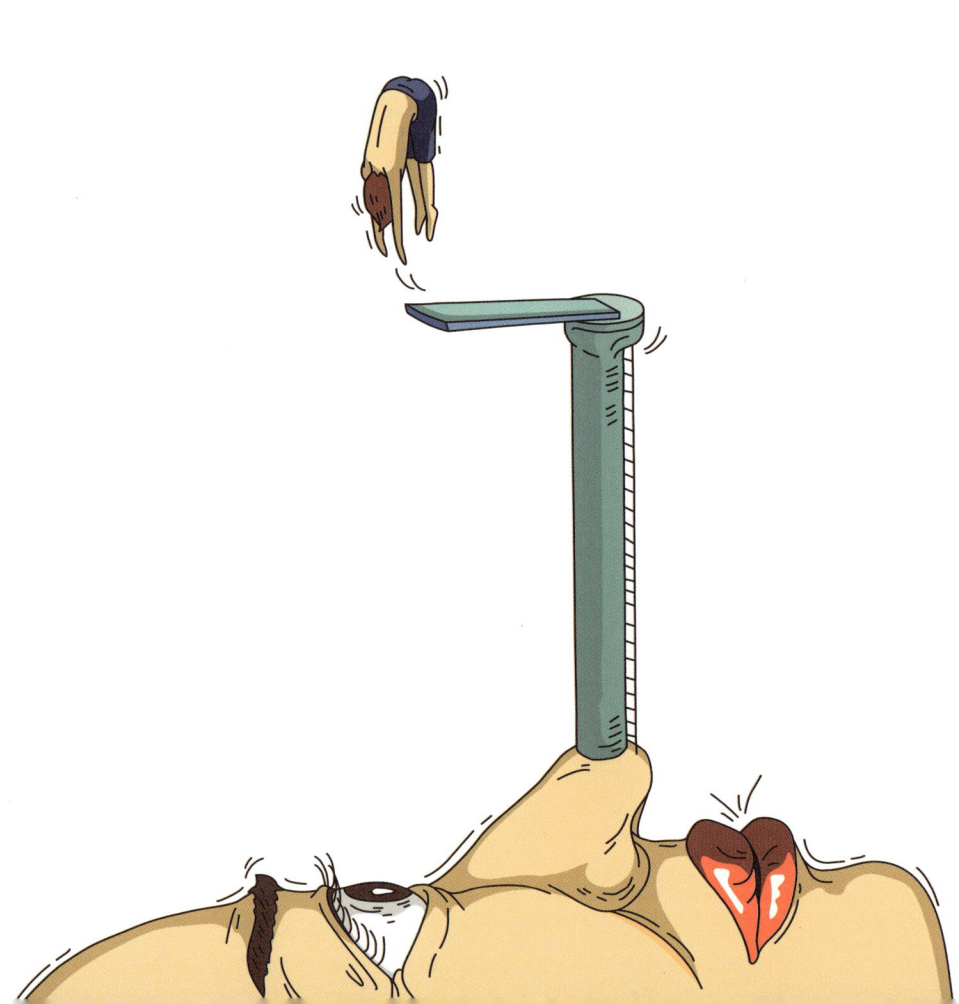

Although "눈에 넣어도 아프지 않다" literally means "to not hurt, even if you put it in your eyes," nearly everything hurts if you put it into your eye; even a speck of dust can irritate your eye. When using this expression, you are implying that you love and care for someone so much that you want to bring them closer and closer to you, so much so that they nearly end up in your eye. For example, to parents and grandparents, their children/grandchildren are incredibly adorable and they love their kin so much that they want to get closer to them to look at them more and more. "Apple of my eye" is a simlar English idiom.

A: 우리 딸 사진 봤어요? 너무 예쁘죠.
　　B: 딸이 그렇게 예뻐요?
A: 그럼요. 눈에 넣어도 아프지 않아요.

A: Have you seen my daughter's photo? She's so pretty, isn't she?
　　B: You love your daughter so dearly?
A: Of course. I could even put her in my eyes and it wouldn't hurt.

A: 책상에 여자 친구 사진밖에 없네요.
　　B: 제 여자 친구 너무 예쁘죠?
A: 그렇게 좋아요?
　　B: 네. 눈에 넣어도 아프지 않을 정도예요.

A: All you have on your desk are photos of your girlfriend.
　　B: My girlfriend is so pretty, right?
A: Do you like her that much?
　　B: Yes, she's so pretty in my eyes.

CHAPTER. 43

가시 = thorn; prickle; fish bone
방석 = sitting mat; sitting cushion

가시방석
[**ga-si-bang-seok**]

LITERAL TRANSLATION:

a sitting mat with thorns

ACTUAL USAGE:

a very uncomfortable situation

There's no such thing as a "sitting mat with thorns" because it would be so painful and uncomfortable. Therefore, "가시방석" is used when you are in an uncomfortable or unfavorable situation, such as when you are being criticized and everyone seems to be angry with you or hate you, you can say, "가시방석에 앉아 있는 것 같았어요" when you are later describing the situation to someone else.

A: 아... 완전 가시방석이네.
　　B: 왜 그래?
A: 선생님이 시험 끝나고 교무실로 오래.
　　B: 근데 왜?
A: 시험 볼 때 컨닝했거든.

A: I feel so uncomfortable and anxious now.
　　B: What's up?
A: My teacher told me to come to the teacher's room after the exam.
　　B: But why?
A: I cheated during the exam.

A: 집에 무슨 일 있어?
　　B: 엄마랑 아빠랑 싸우기 직전이야.
A: 진짜?
　　B: 응. 집에 있는 거 완전 가시방석이야.

A: Is there something wrong at home?
　　B: Mom and Dad are about to fight.
A: Really?
　　B: Yeah, being at home now is so uncomfortable.

CHAPTER. 44

동네 = neighborhood
북 = drum

동네북

[**dong-ne-buk**]

LITERAL TRANSLATION:
a neighborhood drum

ACTUAL USAGE:
someone who gets easily teased by many people;
someone who is often blamed for things

"동네북" literally means "neighborhood drum," which does not make any sense unless you are talking about a musical instrument that is available to anyone and everyone in the neighborhood to beat. Idiomatically, 동네북 is an expression that describes someone who is, figuritively, beat on by everyone; a person who is an easy target for everyone, who gets easily teased by many people, or gets blamed for things quite often, similar to the English idiomatic use of the phrase "that person is a doormat" or the word "scapegoat."

A: 사장님은 항상 저한테만 뭐라고 해요.

B: 그러게요. 이번에는 수진 씨 잘못도 아닌데요.

A: 제가 동네북이에요.

A: The boss always gets mad at only me.

B: Yeah. This time, it wasn't even your fault, Sujin.

A: I'm everybody's punching bag.

A: 경희 씨 왜 또 울어요?

B: 과장님이 별것도 아닌 거 가지고 또 혼냈어요.

A: 또요? 왜요?

B: 부장님한테 혼나고 괜히 경희 씨한테 화풀이하는 거죠.

A: 아휴... 경희 씨가 동네북이네.

A: Why is Kyung-hee crying again?

B: The section chief scolded her again for some small matter.

A: Again? Why?

B: He got scolded by the manager, so he's taking it out on Kyung-hee.

A: (Sigh) She's the punching bag.

CHAPTER. 45

콩깍지 = bean pod, pea pod
쓰다 = to wear; to put on
씌다 is a passive form of 쓰다. 씌다's
subject is always an inanimate object
that is worn or is put on by a human.

콩깍지가 씌다

[kong-kkak-jji-ga ssui-da]

LITERAL TRANSLATION:

a bean pod has been put on

ACTUAL USAGE:

to be so in love that they think
the other person has no flaws

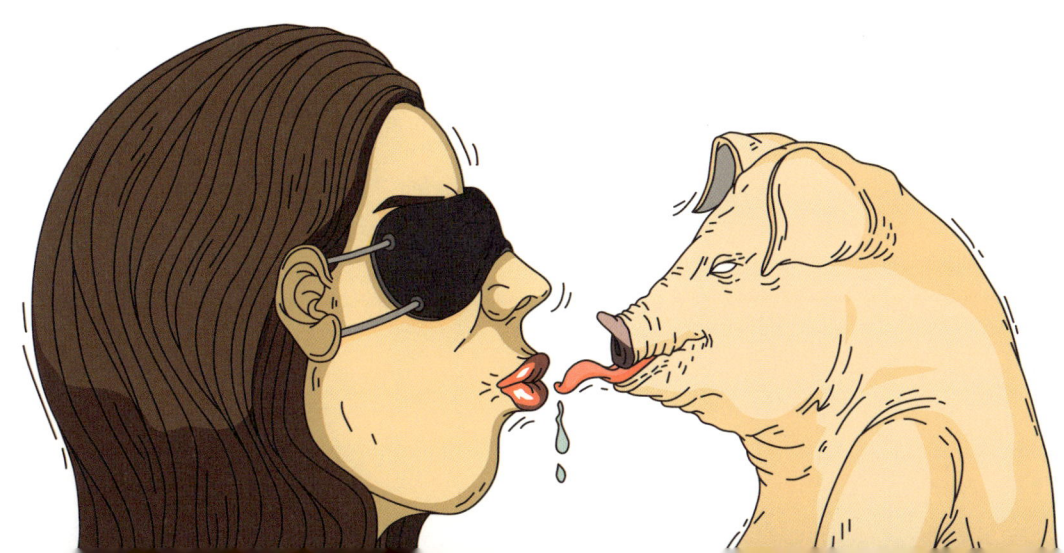

The expression, **콩깍지가 씌다**, is used to describe someone who is helplessly in love. When someone is in love, sometimes they only see the other person's good points, and think that the other person is perfect with no flaws. Sometimes they even make decisions without thinking rationally. In that case, you can say that person is **"콩깍지가 씌었다"** (past tense).

A: 넌 정희가 왜 그렇게 좋아?

　　B: 예쁘고 성격도 좋아서.

A: 예뻐? 안 예쁜데. 그리고 성격도 안 좋던데?

　　B: 아니야. 알고 보면 얼마나 착한데.

A: 콩깍지가 제대로 씌었구나.

A: You like Jeong-hee that much?

　　B: Because she's pretty and has a nice personality.

A: Pretty? She's not really pretty. And she doesn't have a good personality, either.

　　B: You're wrong. When you get to know her, she's really nice.

A: You're really blinded by love.

A: 경환 씨랑 가영 씨랑 사귀는 거 알아요?

　　B: 진짜요? 경환 씨 소문 안 좋던데...

A: 가영 씨는 모르는 거 같아요. 경환 씨 바람둥이라는 소문이 있는데...

　　B: 콩깍지가 씌면 아무도 못 말려요.

A: Do you know that Kyung-hwan and Gayeong are dating?

　　B: Really? I've heard bad rumors about Kyung-hwan.

A: Gayeong doesn't seem to know. There's a rumor that Kyung-hwan is a playboy.

　　B: If you're blinded by love, no one can stop you.

CHAPTER. 46

기 = one's energy;
one's confidence; one's spriit
죽다 = to die

기가 죽다
[gi-ga juk-da]

LITERAL TRANSLATION:
One's energy dies.

ACTUAL USAGE:
to lose one's confidence/energy
and feel depressed

The Sino-Korean word 기 can be translated many different ways depending on the context of the sentence. In this expression, the word "기" is influence by the Chinese word "氣," or "chi," meaning "spirit" or "energy." When paired up with the verb "죽다," which means "to die," you get the feeling that "one's confidence/energy has died." 기가 죽다 is used when comparing yourself to others who think they are better than you at something. The more you think about it, the more you lose confidence in your abilities. The phrase can also be used when being scolded by someone and you become down-trodden. 기가 죽다 is always negative, and as a word of encouragement, people will often say "기죽지 마세요" meaning "don't lose your confidence" or "don't feel bad."

A: 오늘 공연은 정말 잘해야 돼!

    B: 연습 많이 했는데도 떨려요.

A: 기가 죽으면 안 돼.

A: We must do well in today's performance.

    B: I practiced a lot, but I'm still nervous.

A: You shouldn't be overwhelmed and discouraged.

A: 오늘 달리기 시합이 있는데 하필 반에서 제일 잘 달리는 애랑 시합하게 됐어요.

    B: 기죽지 마. 열심히 하면 돼.

A: 아휴... 정말 걱정이에요.

A: I am running in a race today and, of all people, I am going to be running against the best runner in the class.

    B: Don't be discouraged. Just do your best and you'll be fine.

A: (Sigh) I'm so worried.

CHAPTER. 47

눈 = eye
빛 = light
보다 = to look, to see, to watch
알다 = to know

눈빛만 봐도 알다
[nun-bin-man bwa-do al-da]

LITERAL TRANSLATION:
to know by just looking at one's eyes

ACTUAL USAGE:
to be so close to someone
that they can finish each other's sentences;
two people are close enough to each other
that they know what the other is thinking just
by looking at the other's eyes

눈빛 is used to describe the feeling that one's eyes give off. "눈빛이 빛나다" means that someone's "eyes are sparkling/twinkling/shiny" with delight. If someone says "눈빛이 무섭다," it means that someone's "eyes are scary/fierce." These phrases can be used literally, but the expression 눈빛만 봐도 알다 cannot be used in such a literal sense, as it refers to two people being so close/connected with one another that one person can tell what the other person wants or is trying to say just by looking at the other's eyes.

A: 성미 씨, 오늘 삼겹살에 소주 어때요?

B: 제가 오늘 소주 한잔하고 싶은 거 어떻게 알았어요?

A: 전 성미 씨 눈빛만 봐도 알아요.

A: Seongmi, how about samgyeopsal and soju today?

B: How did you know that I wanted to have some soju today?

A: I can just look at your eyes and see what you want.

A: 오늘은 효연 씨한테 데이트 신청할 거야.

B: 짝사랑 그만하고 진짜 용기를 내 봐.

A: 짝사랑 아니야. 효연 씨도 나한테 관심이 있다고.

B: 니가 어떻게 알아?

A: 효연 씨 눈빛만 봐도 다 알아. 나를 좋아하고 있다고.

A: I'm going to ask Hyoyeon out.

B: Stop just having a crush and really summon up some courage.

A: It's not a crush. She's interested in me, too.

B: How do you know?

A: I just have to look at her eyes and I know it. She likes me.

CHAPTER. 48

속 = inside; one's internal thoughts or feelings
썩다 = to be rotten; to rot
썩이다 is a causative form of 썩다.
If you cause something
to rot or make something rot,
you can use the form 썩이다 instead of 썩다.

속을 썩이다

[so-geul sseo-gi-da]

LITERAL TRANSLATION:
to make one's feelings rot

ACTUAL USAGE:
to cause a lot of trouble
and make someone worry a lot

The dictionary defintion for 속 is "inside" or "interior," but it is often used to mean "one's internal thoughts or feelings" in spoken Korean. The causative form of 썩다 (썩이다) is used in this idiom to signify that someone or something is causing a person to worry so much that his/her internal feelings are rotting and causing him/her to suffer. If something is literally rotting inside you, your body will suffer and you will start to feel sick, but luckily this phrase is an idiom and is typically used by parents to express how much worrying they do about their children. If you fail a class at university, one of your parents might say "속을 썩이다!" You can also use this when a machine is broken or continually breaks down.

A: 무슨 일 있어요?

　　B: 오늘 제 아들 학교에 다녀왔어요.

A: 왜요? 또 싸웠대요?

　　B: 네. 제 속을 썩이네요.

A: Is anything wrong?

　　B: I went to my son's school today.

A: Why? He got into a fight again?

　　B: Yeah, he keeps causing trouble and making me worried.

A: 너 성적이 이게 뭐야? 반에서 꼴찌?

　　B: 전 열심히 했어요.

A: 열심히 했다고? 매일 노래방만 갔잖아.

　　B: 엄마, 저 공부하기 싫어요. 가수 되는 게 꿈이에요.

A: 너 자꾸 엄마 속 썩일 거야?

A: Look at your grades. What's this? Last place in your class?

　　B: I studied hard.

A: You studied hard? You only went to the singing room every day.

　　B: Mom, I don't want to study. My dream is to become a singer.

A: Are you going to continue to make me worry?

속을 썩이다

136

CHAPTER. 49

손 = hand
발 = foot
되다 = to become
빌다 = to beg;
to apologize; to pray

손이 발이 되게 빌다
[so-ni ba-ri doe-ge bil-da]

LITERAL TRANSLATION:
to beg/apologize until one's hands become feet

ACTUAL USAGE:
to beg or apologize very sincerely
(by rubbing one's hands)

In Korean culture, if you need to beg for forgiveness from someone for something, like damaging a priceless family heirloom or getting in trouble with the teacher, the action of begging is commonly associated with rubbing your hands together. 손이 발이 되게 빌다 is describing the action of having to rub your hands together so hard in apology that they become ugly like your feet. (If you need a visual reference for this, it can be seen in the dance for the song "Sorry Sorry" by Super Junior.)

A: 여자 친구랑 화해했어요?

    B: 아니요. 손이 발이 되게 빌어도 소용이 없네요.

A: 아휴... 그러니까 왜 바람을 피워요.

A: Did you reconcile with your girlfriend?

    B: No. I begged for forgiveness, but it's not working.

A: (Sigh) So you shouldn't have cheated in the first place.

A: 이거 비싼 옷 아니야? 어떻게 샀어?

    B: 아빠가 학원비 하라고 준 돈으로 샀어.

A: 정말? 어떻게 하려고?

    B: 집에 가서 손이 발이 되게 빌어야지.

A: Aren't these clothes expensive? How did you buy them?

    B: I bought them with the money that my father gave me to pay for my private institute lessons.

A: Really? What are you going to do?

    B: I'm going to beg for forgiveness when I go home.

CHAPTER. 50

바닥 = floor; bottom
나다 = (something) comes out;
to occur; to grow

바닥이 나다

[ba-da-gi na-da]

LITERAL TRANSLATION:

The bottom comes out.

ACTUAL USAGE:

to be out of something

"**바닥**" is the Korean word for the "bottom" or "floor" of something, and the word **나다** means "to come out." Put the words together to form "**바닥이 나다,**" and it literally means "the floor has come out," but it is colloquially understood as "to have nothing left" or something "ran out so I can see the bottom." For example, you have a wallet that is full of money, but you keep spending it until you can see the bottom of your wallet. You can then say, "**돈이 바닥이 났어요,**" meaning that you have no money left. This can be used with anything that is of limited supply: time, money, energy, ideas, etc.

A: 아저씨, 아이스크림 없어요?
　　B: 아, 죄송해요. 오늘 날씨가 더워서 바닥이 났어요.
A: 정말 먹고 싶었는데...

A: You don't have any ice cream?
　　B: I'm sorry. The weather is hot today so we ran out of it.
A: I really wanted to eat some...

A: 오늘 몇 시까지 문 열어요?
　　B: 오늘은 곧 문 닫을 거예요.
A: 벌써요?
　　B: 네. 물건이 다 바닥났어요.

A: Until what time are you open today?
　　B: We're going to close soon for the day.
A: Already?
　　B: Yes. We've sold all our stuff.

CHAPTER. 51

품절 = out of stock
남 = male
여/녀 = female

• • • • • • • •

품절남 / 품절녀

[pum-jeol-lam] / [pum-jeol-lyeo]

LITERAL TRANSLATION:

sold-out man / sold-out woman

ACTUAL USAGE:

(newly) married man / (newly) married woman;
off the market

"남" (男) and "여/녀" (女) are Sino-Korean words for "male" and "female," respectively. (When the word 녀 is the initial letter of a word, it becomes "여" for ease of pronunciation.) 품절남 and 품절녀 are relatively new slang terms that literally mean "out of stock male/female" and are commonly used to refer to recently married individuals. These terms are very rarely used in the same way as the English expression "off the market," which can refer to someone who has a newly acquired boy/girlfriend.

A: 은애 씨, 저 청첩장 나왔어요.

　　B: 진짜요? 이제 곧 품절남 되는 거예요?

A: 네. 저도 품절남이에요.

A: Eun-ae, I had my wedding invitations made.

　　B: Really? You're going off the market?

A: Yeah. I'm going to be sold out (married).

A: 우와, 저 여자 진짜 예쁘다. 누구야?

　　B: 몰라도 돼. 어차피 품절녀야.

A: 진짜? 아쉽다.

A: Wow. That girl is really pretty. Who is she?

　　B: You don't have to know. She's married anyway.

A: Really? That's too bad.

CHAPTER. 52

머리 = head; hair
피 = blood
마르다 = to dry; to be dried

머리에 피도 안 마르다

[meo-ri-e pi-do an ma-reu-da]

LITERAL TRANSLATION:
the blood on one's head hasn't dried up yet

ACTUAL USAGE:
to be wet behind the ears

145

"머리에 피도 안 마르다" literally means "even the blood on your head hasn't dried up yet," insinuating that a person is too young and inexperienced to be doing something or acting a certain way (rude or arrogant). It is always used in a negative way and is often said as "머리에 피도 안 마른 게!" to mean "how dare you try to do this/challenge me!" This expression cannot be casually used in the same way as the English phrase "still wet behind the ears," so be careful when using this Korean idiom!

A: 너 몇 살이야?

　　B: 왜요? 아저씨가 알아서 뭐 하게요?

A: 이 머리에 피도 안 마른 게 말버릇이 그게 뭐야?

A: How old are you?

　　B: Why? Why do you want to know that?

A: You're still wet behind the ears. Why are you so rude?

A: 너 지금 나이가 몇 살인데 벌써 여자를 사귀어?

　　B: 아빠, 저 벌써 중학생이에요.

A: 중학생은 한창 공부해야 할 나이잖아.

　　B: 제 친구들 모두 여자 친구 있어요.

A: 머리에 피도 안 마른 것들이 벌써 연애야!

A: You're too young to be dating a girl already.

　　B: Dad, I'm already a middle school student.

A: Middle school students are supposed to be studying a lot.

　　B: All my friends have a girlfriend.

A: You guys are still wet behind the ears and you are already dating girls?

CHAPTER. 53

비행기 = airplane
타다 = to ride; to get on (a vehicle);
to take (a bus/subway/taxi)
태우다 is a causative form of 타다.

· · · · ·

비행기 태우다
[bi-haeng-gi tae-u-da]

LITERAL TRANSLATION:

to get someone on a plane

ACTUAL USAGE:

to praise someone a lot

147

In English, the phrase "give someone a big head" means "to flatter someone excessively" or "to give a lot of praise." "비행기 태우다" has the same idiomatic meaning, but the literal translation is "to get someone on an airplane" which insinuates that you are making someone feel really happy about themselves, as if they are "walking on air" or "flying high" from too many compliments.

A: 우와, 준하 씨 오늘 너무 멋있다.
B: 머리 스타일 바꿨는데 괜찮아요?
A: 진짜 잘 어울려. 영화 배우 같아.
B: 에이~ 괜히 비행기 태우지 마세요.

A: Wow. Junha, you look amazing today.
B: I changed my hairstyle. Does it look okay?
A: It looks great on you. You look like a movie star.
B: Come on, don't flatter me.

A: 지영 씨가 태성 씨 칭찬을 많이 하던데?
B: 지영 씨가요? 뭐라고요?
A: 태성 씨 매너 좋다고. 지영 씨가 좋아하나?
B: 그럴 리가 없어요. 비행기 태우지 마세요.

A: Jiyeong was speaking highly of you, Taeseong.
B: Jiyeong did? What did she say?
A: She said that you have good manners. Perhaps she likes you?
B: That's impossible. Don't flatter me.

CHAPTER. 54

바가지 = large plastic bowl;
a bowl made out of a gourd
쓰다 = to wear; to put on; to use; to write

바가지 쓰다
[ba-ga-ji sseu-da]

LITERAL TRANSLATION:
to put on a large bowl

ACTUAL USAGE:
to get ripped off

This expression originates from a gambling game which was introduced to Korea about 100 years ago. The host of the game would place 10 bowls upside down on a surface and number the bowls one through ten. The host would then think of a number between one and ten and have the players (usually one or two) place their bets on the bowl they thought the host was thinking of. If the players bet on the right bowl, they win their money back. If they lose, the host collected the money and all that is left is the empty bowl which was bet on. "바가지 쓰다," or "wearing a bowl," became a symbol of getting swindled by the host of the game. Similary, when you are ripped off or deliberately overcharged for something because you didn't know the original cost or you had no other option but to buy the item, you can say "바가지 썼어요" after you realize you were swindled.

A: 아무래도 바가지 쓴 것 같아요.

    B: 왜요?

A: 친구 아는 사람이라고 해서 컴퓨터를 샀거든요. 그런데 비싸게 산 것 같아요.

A: I'm afraid it looks like I've been ripped off.

    B: Why?

A: My friend said he knows this guy, so I bought a computer from him. But I think I paid too much.

A: 이거 얼마에 샀어요?

    B: 이거요? 3만원에 샀어요.

A: 3만원이요? 이거 보통 5천원밖에 안 해요.

    B: 그럼 저 바가지 쓴 거예요?

A: How much did you pay for it?

    B: This? I got it for 30,000 won.

A: 30,000 won? It usually only costs 5,000 won.

    B: Then did I get ripped off?

CHAPTER. 55

하나 = one (native Korean number)
한 is the adjective form of 하나.
눈 = eye
팔다 = to sell

한눈팔다
[han-nun-pal-da]

LITERAL TRANSLATION:
to sell one eye

ACTUAL USAGE:
to get distracted;
to not concentrate on one thing

"한눈팔다" literally means "to sell an eye," but used as an idiom, it means "to take one's eyes off (something)" or "to become distracted." For example, when you are trying to concentrate on your studies, but you find a funny YouTube video to watch or your cell phone rings and you look away from your books, you are "한눈팔다."

A: 저 커플 싸웠어? 둘이 따로 왔네.
　　B: 얘기 못 들었어? 헤어졌대.
A: 정말? 왜?
　　B: 여자가 한눈팔았대.

A: Did that couple fight? They came here separately.
　　B: You didn't hear about it? I heard they split up.
A: Really? Why?
　　B: The girl became interested in another man.

A: 오늘은 제가 차로 집까지 데려다줄게요.
　　B: 괜찮아요. 혼자 갈게요.
A: 왜요? 차로 가면 편하잖아요.
　　B: 운전할 때 항상 한눈팔잖아요. 불안해서 싫어요.

A: I will give you a ride back home toady.
　　B: I'm okay. I can go by myself.
A: Why? It's convenient to go by car.
　　B: You always lose concentration and look at other things while driving. I don't like it because I feel anxious.

CHAPTER. 56

수박 = watermelon
겉 = outside; exterior
핥다 = to lick

수박 겉핥기

[su-bak geot hal-kki]

LITERAL TRANSLATION:

to lick the outside of a watermelon

ACTUAL USAGE:

to do something superficially

"수박 겉핥기" is similar to the English expression "only scratching at the surface." By only licking the outside of a watermelon (the rind), you will never taste the juicy and delicious fruit of the watermelon. The same goes for reading a book: if you just look at the cover or skim the text, you won't ever "taste" what's inside. Using 수박 겉핥기 to describe someone's actions is the same way as saying he/she is doing it half-heartedly. You will often see and hear this phrase used as "수박 겉핥기 식으로," meaning "(doing something) in a superficial way." However, you may also hear people omit the first word, 수박, and only say "겉핥기," which still carries the same meaning as the full expression.

A: 아휴... 자격증 또 못 땄어.

B: 항상 수박 겉핥기 하듯이 대충 공부하니까 그러지.

A: 아니야. 이번엔 그래도 절반은 공부했어.

A: (Sigh) I failed my certificate exam again.

B: That's because you always study half-heartedly, like licking the surface of a watermelon.

A: No. This time I studied half of it, at least.

A: 제가 쓴 시나리오 읽어 봤어요?

B: 네. 괜찮은 거 같아요. 슬픈 사랑 이야기 좋아해요.

A: 네? 수박 겉핥기 식으로 읽은 거 아니에요? 처음에는 슬픈 이야기지만 결론은 해피엔딩이라고요.

A: Did you read the scenario I wrote?

B: Yeah, I think it's good. I like sad love stories.

A: What? Did you just skim through it? It's a sad story in the beginning, but the ending is happy.

CHAPTER. 57

도마 = cutting board
위 = on; above
오르다 = to climb; to go up; to ascent

도마 위에 오르다
[do-ma wi-e o-reu-da]

LITERAL TRANSLATION:
to get on a cutting board

ACTUAL USAGE:
to be at the heart of a debate;
to be publicly put on the chopping block

In English, when someone is up for elimination or is bound to be cut, it is said that person is "on the chopping block." 도마 위에 오르다 has a similar meaning, but suggests that the person has become a problem and/or is at the heart of a debate. This expression is never used in a cheerful manner to describe something good or positive.

A: 회사 분위기 왜 이래?

B: 지난달 마무리 된 프로젝트 때문에 그래.

A: 그거 사장님한테 칭찬받은 거잖아.

B: 비리가 있다는 소문이 있어서 도마 위에 올랐어.

A: Why is the atmosphere like this in the company?

B: It's because of the project that was finished last month.

A: The boss complimented it, didn't he?

B: Rumor has it that there was some corruption, so it's being criticized now.

A: 이 기사 봤어?

B: 이 사람 유명한 교수잖아. 이 사람이 왜 갑자기 도마 위에 올랐어?

A: 논문을 직접 쓴 게 아니라는 소문이 돌고 있대.

A: Did you see this article?

B: He's a famous professor. Why is he suddenly being criticized?

A: There are rumors that he didn't write his thesis himself.

CHAPTER. 58

딸 = daughter
바보 = fool, idiot

딸바보
[ttal-ba-bo]

LITERAL TRANSLATION:
daughter idiot

ACTUAL USAGE:
parent who loves and praises his/her daughter
so much that the daughter can do anything
she wants or she is overprotected

You can call someone a "딸바보" if he/she is the type of parent who always talks about how cute his/her daughter is to other people, who rarely scolds the daughter and is overly nice, or a parent who is overprotective. 딸바보 can be the mom or dad, or both, but most of the time, it's used to describe a dad. Even though there are many parents who act this way with their son, the word 아들바보 is not as widely used as 딸바보. The English phrase "daddy's little girl" has an identical meaning.

A: 제가 우리 딸 사진 보여줬어요?
　　B: 그럼요. 많이 봤어요.
A: 우리 딸 천재인 거 같아요. 말을 정말 잘해요.
　　B: 아휴... 진짜 딸바보인 거 알아요?

A: Did I show you my daughter's picture?
　　B: Sure. I've seen it often.
A: I think my daughter is a genius. She speaks really well.
　　B: (Sigh) Do you know that you become really shamelss when you
　　　　praise your daughter?

A: 인혜 씨, 임신했다면서요? 너무 축하해요.
　　B: 네. 고마워요.
A: 딸이에요? 아들이에요?
　　B: 딸이요. 벌써 너무 기대돼요. 얼마나 예쁠지 상상이
　　　　안 돼요.
A: 벌써요? 벌써부터 딸바보 될 준비하는 거예요?

A: Inhye, I heard you got pregnant! Congratulations!
　　B: Yes, thank you.
A: Daughter or son?
　　B: It's a daughter. I'm already looking forward to it. I can't imagine
　　　　how pretty she will be.
A: Already? You're already preparing to start praising your daughter?

CHAPTER. 59

발 = foot
넓다 = to be wide

발이 넓다

[ba-ri neol-tta]

LITERAL TRANSLATION:

to have wide feet

ACTUAL USAGE:

to be well connected

"발이 넓다" literally means "to have wide feet," but if used figuratively, it means that a person has a wide network; he/she knows a lot of people and has a broad base of support. If you literally want to say that someone has large feet, you would say "발이 크다."

A: 은주 씨 생일 파티에 가요?

   B: 네. 생일 파티 빨리 가고 싶어요.

A: 왜요?

   B: 은주 씨가 발이 넓거든요. 예쁜 친구들이 많을 거 같아요.

A: Are you going to Eunju's birthday party?

   B: Yeah. I want to go to the birthday party really soon.

A: Why?

   B: Eunju knows a lot of people. I think she has many pretty friends.

A: 주변에 여행사 다니는 친구 혹시 없어요?

   B: 있어요. 왜요? 어디 가려고요?

A: 부모님 여행시켜 드리려고요. 태훈 씨는 발이 진짜 넓네요. 저는 여행사 다니는 친구 한 명도 없는데.

A: Do you know anyone around you that works at a travel agency?

   B: I do. Why? Are you going somewhere?

A: I want to send my parents on a trip. Taehun, you really know a lot of people. I don't know anyone who works at a travel agency.

CHAPTER. 60

눈 = eye
높다 = to be high

눈이 높다
[nu-ni nop-tta]

LITERAL TRANSLATION:
to have high eyes

ACTUAL USAGE:
to have a high standard when choosing something;
to be picky

Obviously, physically having "high eyes" doesn't make much sense, so this term is used to describe someone who has high expectations or is quite picky. More often than not, you will find that 눈이 높다 is used when someone is listing qualities that he/she is looking for in a relationship partner. The expression can also be used when someone has ridiculously high standards about other things, such as cleanliness, quality of work, food taste, etc.

A: 상학 씨는 성격도 좋은데 왜 여자 친구가 없을까?

B: 성격 좋지. 근데 눈이 높다는 소문이 있어.

A: 그래? 어쩐지.

A: Sang-hak has a nice personality. Why doesn't he have a girlfriend?

B: He does have a nice personality. But rumor has it that he has high standards for girls.

A: Really? No wonder.

A: 내 친구 소개해 줄까?

B: 필요 없어. 전에도 예쁜 친구 소개해 준다고 했는데 이상했다고.

A: 네가 눈이 높은 거야. 다들 예쁘다고 하는데 너만 이상하다고 하는 거야.

A: Do you want me to introduce you to someone?

B: No, thanks. You said you would introduce me to a pretty girl last time, and she wasn't pretty at all.

A: It's just that you have high standards. Everybody says she's pretty and you alone say she's not.

CHAPTER. 61

귀 = ear
얇다 = to be thin

귀가 얇다
[gwi-ga yal-tta]

LITERAL TRANSLATION:
to have thin ears

ACTUAL USAGE:
impressionable;
easily swayed by the opinion of others

"귀가 얇다" literally means "to have thin ears," but as an idiomatic expression, it means that someone is naive, gullible, or impressionable; someone who is easily influenced by what he/she is told. For example, a 귀가 얇은 사람 (person with thin ears) might fall prey to a goofy sales pitch or frequently change his/her opinion based on what other people are saying.

A: 은서 씨, 휴가 그리스로 간다고 하지 않았어요? 이탈리아 여행 정보를 왜 보고 있어요?

　　B: 채은 씨가 최근에 이탈리아 갔다 왔는데 정말 좋았대요.

A: 그리스도 친구가 좋다고 해서 간다고 했잖아요.

　　B: 제가 귀가 좀 얇아요.

A: Eunseo, didn't you say that you were going on vacation to Greece? Why are you looking at information about traveling to Italy?

*　　B: Chae-eun recently went to Italy and she said she had a great time.*

A: You said that you were going to Greece because your friend also said it was good.

*　　B: I am easily influenced by other people's opinions.*

A: 홈쇼핑 또 했어요? 오늘은 뭐예요?

　　B: 화장품을 너무 싸게 팔잖아요. 이거 바르면 송혜교 피부가 될 수 있대요.

A: 진짜 귀가 너무 얇은 거 아니에요?

　　B: 아니에요. 한 번 써 봤는데 진짜 좋았어요.

A: You bought stuff from home shopping again? What is it today?

*　　B: They were selling cosmetics at such a cheap price. They say that if you use this, you can have a skin like Song Hye-gyo's.*

A: Don't you think you are too gullible?

*　　B: No, I tried it once and it was really good.*

CHAPTER. 62

하늘과 땅 차이
[ha-neul-gwa ttang cha-i]

LITERAL TRANSLATION:
the difference between the sky and the ground

ACTUAL USAGE:
to be completely different;
to have huge gap between levels

When using this expression, you are describing the vast difference between two things, abilities, or levels, just as there is a very large distance between the ground and the sky.

A: 회사 이직하니까 어때요?

   B: 너무 좋아요. 지금 회사는 직원 복지가 아주 좋아요.

A: 전에 회사도 좋지 않았어요?

   B: 네? 아니요. 하늘과 땅 차이예요.

A: How do you feel to have changed jobs?

   B: I feel great. My new job has really good benefits.

A: Didn't your previous job have good benefits as well?

   B: What? No. It's a world of difference.

A: 형식이 요즘 정말 많이 변했죠?

   B: 예전에 비교하면 정말 하늘과 땅 차이예요.

A: 정말 많이 변해서 깜짝깜짝 놀래요.

A: Hyeongsik has changed a lot recently, right?

   B: Compared to before, he's completely different.

A: He's changed so much that I am continually surprised.

CHAPTER. 63

기분 = feeling; emotion
가라앉다 = to sink; to go under

기분이 가라앉다
[gi-bu-ni ga-ra-an-tta]

LITERAL TRANSLATION:
One's feelings have sunk.

ACTUAL USAGE:
to feel depressed

Similar to the English expressions "down in the dumps" or "feeling blue," 기분이 가라앉다 implies a feeling of sadness, but as a result of being let down or something coming into mind that makes you have a "sunken feeling." For example: you were so happy that you received the highest grade in the class on an exam that you ran home to tell your mom, but instead, your mother told you that a relative has passed away. In that moment, "기분이 가라앉다."

A: 경희 씨, 오늘 안 좋은 일 있어요?

B: 모르겠어요. 갑자기 기분이 가라앉았어요.

A: 오늘 비도 오고 날도 추워서 그런가 봐요. 우리 따뜻한 거 마시러 갈래요?

A: Kyung-hee, is there anything wrong today?

B: I don't know. I suddenly feel down.

A: Maybe because it's raining and cold. Do you want to go get something warm to drink?

A: 오늘 계속 기분이 가라앉네.

B: 왜? 무슨 일 있어?

A: 어제 과장님이 한마디 했거든요. 계속 신경 쓰여요.

B: 잊어버려. 오늘 술 한 잔 할래?

A: I've felt terrible all day today.

B: Why? Something wrong?

A: The section chief got upset at me yesterday. I can't stop thinking about it.

B: Forget about it. Do you want to have a drink later today?

CHAPTER. 64

날아가다 = to fly away

날아갈 것 같다

[na-ra-gal geot gat-tta]

LITERAL TRANSLATION:
to feel like one's flying away

ACTUAL USAGE:
to feel extremly happy; overjoyed

날아갈 것 같다 literally means "I think I'm going to fly." Unfortunately, humans do not have the ability to flap their arms and fly, so this expression is used when someone is extremely happy or overjoyed about something. It is used in the same way as the English idioms "walking on air" and "on cloud nine."

A: 시험 끝났다! 아, 날아갈 것 같아!

　　　B: 난 아직 시험 안 끝났어. 내일까지 시험이야.

A: 안됐다. 난 정말 끝! 오늘부터 실컷 잘 거야.

A: The exams are over! I feel like I could fly!

　　　B: My exams are not over yet. I have exams until tomorrow.

A: Too bad. I am completely done with exams. From today, I'm going to sleep all I want.

A: 나 결혼한다.

　　　B: 진짜? 프로포즈 성공했어?

A: 응. 어제 프로포즈 했는데 너무 좋아하더라고. 나도 지금 날아갈 것 같아.

A: I'm getting married.

　　　B: Really? Did you propose succesfully?

A: Yeah. I proposed yesterday and she really liked it. I feel so happy now, too.

CHAPTER. 65

가슴에 못을 박다
[ga-seu-me mo-seul bak-tta]

LITERAL TRANSLATION:

to drive a nail into one's chest

ACTUAL USAGE:

to say something very hurtful to someone;
to do something
that makes someone feel deeply hurt

가슴에 못을 박다 describes the intense feeling one gets when something is said or done that causes a person to feel as if someone is stabbing him/her in the heart. This expression can be used when talking about heart ache or a relationship breakup, but it is used more when someone is very direct, harsh, and unfiltered when speaking to another, or when a child does something and the parent responds "가슴에 못을 박다." A related English colloquialism is, "stab me in the heart, why don't you?!"

A: 울지 마세요.

　　B: 내가 너를 어떻게 키웠는데. 내 가슴에 못을 박는구나.

A: 앞으로 효도하면서 살면 되잖아요. 죄송해요.

A: Don't cry.

　　B: I worked so hard to raise you and you are breaking my heart.

A: I will be a good child from now on. I'm sorry.

A: 헤어져. 나 다른 여자 생겼어.

　　B: 뭐라고? 니가 내 가슴에 못을 박고 행복할 것 같아?

A: 미안해. 나도 어쩔 수가 없었어.

A: Let's break up. I am seeing another girl.

　　B: What? Do you think you can be happy after breaking my heart?

A: I'm sorry. I couldn't help it.

CHAPTER. 66

말 = word(s); language; what one says
쉽다 = to be easy

말은 쉽다

[ma-reun swip-da]

LITERAL TRANSLATION:

Words are easy.

ACTUAL USAGE:

Easier said than done.

Rather than being taken literally as "words are easy," think of "말은 쉽다" as having the same meaning as the English "easier said than done." If a task is easier to talk about than to do, then the words to speak are formed much easier than the action of accomplishing the task.

A: 몇 년 동안 세계 여행 다니는 거 너무 멋지지 않아요?

B: 그게 말은 쉽지 진짜 힘들 거예요.

A: 맞아요. 힘들긴 할 것 같아요.

A: Traveling around the world for years, isn't that awesome?

B: It's easy to say, but it will be very difficult.

A: That's right. I guess it will be difficult.

A: 다이어트가 뭐가 어려워?

B: 니가 해 봐. 진짜 어려워.

A: 저녁 안 먹고, 운동 매일 하면 금방 되잖아.

B: 말은 쉽지. 너도 해 봐.

A: Losing weight is not difficult at all.

B: You try doing it yourself. It's really hard.

A: You just have to skip dinner and exercise every day, then soon you will lose weight.

B: It's easier said than done. You try doing it yourself.

CHAPTER. 67

생각 = thought; idea
없다 = to not exsist;
to not have; to be not there

생각이 없다
[saeng-ga-gi eop-tta]

LITERAL TRANSLATION:

to not have any thoughts

ACTUAL USAGE:

to not to be in the mood for something

"생각이 없다" literally means "to have no thoughts." In everyday Korean, however, it is use figuratively to mean "to not be in the mood (for something)," most often referring to food. For example, you are not hungry and you do not want to eat lunch, but someone asks you why you are not eating, you can reply, "그냥 생각이 없어서요." This expression is also used to describe a person or a behavior, and to blame how inconsiderate and/or how thoughtless they are.

A: 미안해요. 민정 씨가 이렇게 싫어할 줄 몰랐어요.

B: 내가 몇 번이나 말했어요. 정말 생각이 없는 사람 아니에요?

A: 진짜 미안해요. 화 풀어요.

A: I'm sorry, Minjeong. I didn't know you would hate it so much.

B: How many times have I told you? You really don't think, do you?

A: I'm sorry. Please stop being mad at me.

A: 오늘 왜 이렇게 밥을 안 먹어요?

B: 밥 생각이 없네요.

A: 왜요? 맛없어요?

B: 아니요. 아까 간식을 먹어서 그래요.

A: Why are you not eating much today?

B: I don't have an appetite.

A: Why? Is it not delicioius?

B: No. I just had a snack earlier. That's why.

생각이 없다

CHAPTER. 68

한 번 = one time
봐주다 = to turn a blind eye to something;
to cut someone some slack;
to let someone off the hook

한 번 봐주다
[han beon bwa-ju-da]

This phrase means "to let someone off the hook this one time," "to cut someone some slack one time," or "to forgive someone (and to not punish) just this once." You can use 한 번 봐준다 to tell someone that you are going to let him/her off the hook this one time. If you are asking someone to cut you some slack, you can say, "한 번만 봐주세요" ("Please let me off the hook just this once").

A: 선생님 한 번만 봐주세요. 네?
　　B: 내일 부모님 모셔 와.
A: 진짜 잘못했어요. 반성하고 있어요.

A: Teacher, please forgive me this once, will you?
　　B: Bring your parents tomorrow.
A: I'm so sorry. I am regretting what I did.

A: 미안, 미안. 차가 너무 막혀서 늦었어.
　　B: 왜 매일 차가 막혀!
A: 진짜 미안해. 내가 저녁 살게. 한 번만 봐줘.
　　B: 다음에는 늦지 마.

A: I'm sorry. I am late because the traffic was bad.
　　B: Why are you always stuck in traffic?
A: I'm so sorry. I'll buy dinner. Please forgive me this once.
　　B: Don't be late next time.

CHAPTER. 69

넋 = soul; spirit
잃다 = to lose

넋을 잃다

[neok-seul il-ta]

LITERAL TRANSLATION:

to lose one's soul

ACTUAL USAGE:

to space out; to be lost in thought;
to be devastated and be speechless;
to be beside oneself

넋을 잃다 can be used in very different situations, but has the same meaning of "to lose one's soul/spirit": if you received some bad news or are completely devastated by a certain event, it might seem as though you've lost yourself. Alternatively, if you are star-struck when you see your favorite celebrity in person, you may be beside yourself with happiness that you forget to speak or do something out of character that makes it seem like you have "lost your marbles."

A: 뭘 그렇게 넋을 잃고 쳐다봐?

    B: 응? 아... 저기 저 여자 봐 봐. 진짜 예쁘지?

A: 우와~ 진짜 예쁘다. 저 여자 누구야?

A: What are you looking at? You're so absorbed.

    B: What? Oh, look at that girl over there. She's really pretty, right?

A: Wow. She's really pretty. Who is she?

A: 영호 씨, 무슨 일 있어요?

    B: 아버지가 편찮으셔서 병원에 입원하셨대요.

A: 걱정되겠어요. 아주 넋을 잃은 사람 같아요.

A: Yeong-ho, is there anything wrong?

    B: I heard that my father got sick and is hospitalized.

A: You must be worried. You look like you're lost in thought.

CHAPTER. 70

급하다 = to be urgent
돌아가다 = to go back, to return;
to take a detour

급할수록 돌아가라

[geu-pal su-rok do-ra-ga-ra]

LITERAL TRANSLATION:
The more urgent (something is),
the more detours (there are).

ACTUAL USAGE:
The more you rush, the longer it takes.

People often try to find shortcuts when they are in a hurry to make it easier on themselves, but most of the time, things are not done correctly because they are in a rush and no time is saved. Sometimes people need a reminder that it is better to step back, breathe, and take it one step at a time. In Korean, you can advise someone that "haste makes waste" by saying, "급할수록 돌아가라."

A: 정신이 하나도 없네.

    B: 오늘 집들이 때문에 그래?

A: 청소도 해야 하고, 음식도 만들어야 하고, 옷도 갈아입어야 하고. 아...

    B: 급할수록 돌아가라는 말도 있잖아. 하나씩 천천히 해 봐.

A: Things are so busy that they are driving me out of my mind.

    B: Is it because of the house warming party today?

A: I have to clean the house, make the food, and change clothes...

    B: And they say make haste slowly. Do them one by one slowly.

A: 차가 너무 막혀. 어떻게 하지?

    B: 안 막히는 길 찾아볼게. 조금만 기다려 봐.

A: 오늘은 늦으면 정말 안 되는데.

    B: 급할수록 돌아가라고 하잖아. 조급하게 생각하지 말고 안 막히는 길 잘 찾아보자.

A: The traffic is terrible. What should we do?

    B: I will look for a route that doesn't have bad traffic. Wait a second.

A: I really shouldn't be late today.

    B: They say make haste slowly. Let's not think impatiently and try to look for a route that doesn't have bad traffic.

CHAPTER. 71

• • • •

까칠하다

[kka-chi-ra-da]

LITERAL TRANSLATION:

to be rough

ACTUAL USAGE:

to be cranky

까칠하다 can be used literally to describe a multitude of things, but it is commonly used to describe the rough texture of something like sand. Figuratively, 까칠하다 can describe an unfriendly person or a person who has a grumpy disposition or cranky behavior. The phrase used to describe this type of person is "까칠한 사람." By adding the word "굴다," which means "to act or to behave," you can say "까칠하게 굴다" a friend who is in a bad mood and is being cranky.

A: 음악 좀 줄여. 너무 시끄럽잖아.
    B: 알았어. 이제 괜찮지?
A: 좀 조용히 먹을 수 없어?
    B: 오늘 왜 이렇게 까칠해? 무슨 일 있어?

A: Turn the music down, it's too loud.
    B: Okay. It's okay now, right?
A: Can't you eat a little quieter?
    B: Why are you abrasive today? Is anything wrong?

A: 진수 씨가 왜 좋아요?
    B: 매력 있잖아요.
A: 매력이요? 성격이 너무 까칠해서 전 싫어요.
    B: 그게 그 사람 매력이에요. 전 까칠한 사람 너무 좋아요.

A: Why do you like Jinsu?
    B: He's attractive.
A: Attractive? He has a difficult personality, so I don't like him.
    B: That's his charm. I really like people who are abrasive.

CHAPTER. 72

가슴 = heart; chest
오다 = to come
닿다 = to touch; to reach

가슴에 와 닿다
[ga-seu-me wa da-ta]

LITERAL TRANSLATION:
to come along and touch the heart

ACTUAL USAGE:
to hit home; to touch one's heart

If you hear a song, read a story, or watch a movie that really "hits home" or touches your heart, you can use "**가슴에 와 닿다**" to express your feelings. The phrase itself literally means that "(something) comes and touches/reaches your heart," but it is commonly used in colloquial Korean as an idiom.

A: 이 책 읽어 봤어요?

B: 아니요. 아직이요. 어때요?

A: 꼭 읽어 보세요. 가슴에 와 닿는 내용이 정말 많아요.

A: Have you read this book?

B: No. Not yet. How is it?

A: Be sure to read it. It has so many parts that touch your heart.

A: 남자 친구랑 화해했어요?

B: 네. 화해했어요.

A: 어떻게요? 이번에는 절대 용서 안 한다고 했잖아요.

B: 편지를 받았는데 내용이 가슴에 와 닿았어요. 바로 화가 풀어졌어요.

A: Did you reconcile with your boyfriend?

B: Yes, I did.

A: How? You said you weren't going to forgive him this time.

B: I received a letter and what he wrote was touching. I was instantly not mad any more.

가슴에 와 닿다

CHAPTER. 73

눈 = eye
코 = nose
뜨다 = to open
새 = 사이 = gap; space;
during, while; relationship
없다 = to not exist; to not have;
to be not there
바쁘다 = to be busy

눈코 뜰 새 없이 바쁘다

[nun-ko tteul sae eop-si ba-ppeu-da]

LITERAL TRANSLATION:
to be so busy that there's no time
to even open one's eyes and nose

ACTUAL USAGE:
to be very busy

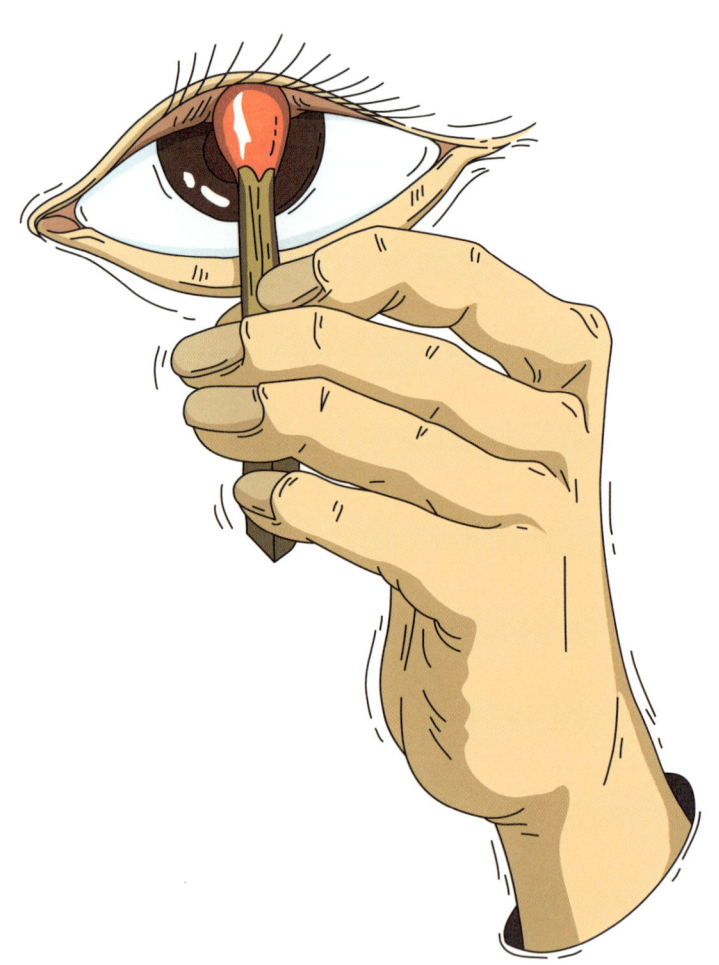

If you translate "눈코 뜰 새 없이 바쁘다" literally, it means "to be so busy that there's no time to open one's eyes and nose." Used idiomatically, it simply means "to be extremely busy," so busy that you don't have time to "stop and smell the roses."

A: 오늘 저녁 영화 예매했죠?
B: 아... 못 했어요.
A: 진짜요? 그 영화 인기 많아서 예매 안 하면 못 보는데...
B: 미안해요. 오늘 정말 눈코 뜰 새 없이 바빴어요.

A: You made reservations for tonight's movie, right?
B: No, I couldn't.
A: Really? That movie is popular, so you can't see it without making reservations.
B: I'm sorry. I've been crazy busy today

A: 요즘 가게 잘돼요?
B: 네. 요즘 눈코 뜰 새 없이 바빠요.
A: 정말 잘됐어요.

A: Is everything going well with your store?
B: Yes. We're super busy these days.
A: That's great.

CHAPTER. 74

눈 = eye
밖 = outside
나다 = to grow; to occur;
to break out;
(something) comes out

눈 밖에 나다

[**nun ba-kke na-da**]

LITERAL TRANSLATION:
to get on the outside of someone's eye

ACTUAL USAGE:
to lose favor with someone

눈 밖에 나다 is somewhat the opposite of 눈에 넣어도 아프지 않다. "눈 밖에" means "outside of the eye," so rather than being in favor with someone so much that he/she wants to keep you close, 눈 밖에 나다 is used when someone does something wrong or he/she did something that was not well-received, therefore falling out of favor and being figuratively pushed away from the eye. This expression is typically used when a younger person, or a person who is in a lower position, does something wrong and loses the favor of an elder or person in a higher position.

A: 기영 씨, 오늘 회식하는 거 알죠?

B: 진짜요? 저 오늘은 회식 못 갈 것 같아요.

A: 오늘 회식에 이사님 오신다고 했어요. 눈 밖에 나면 안 좋을 걸요.

A: Kiyoung, you know that you are having a company dinner today, right?

B: Really? I won't be able to go to the dinner today.

A: I heard the managing director is going to come to the dinner. It wouldn't be good to lose favor with him.

A: 요즘 부장님 나한테 왜 그러지?

B: 왜?

A: 자꾸 시비 걸고 뭐라고 하시네.

B: 부장님 눈 밖에 난 거 아냐?

A: Why is the manager treating me like that these days?

B: Why?

A: He's always finding faults in my work and gets mad at me.

B: Perhaps you've lost his trust?

CHAPTER. 75

마음 = mind; heart
없다 = to not exist; to not have;
to be not there
말 = word(s); language;
what one says

마음에도 없는 말을 하다
[ma-eu-me-do eom-neun ma-reul ha-da]

LITERAL TRANSLATION:
to say something that is not even in one's heart

ACTUAL USAGE:
to say something and not mean it;
to apologize half-heartedly

Saying something that you do not mean, or offering an apology half-heartedly, is the meaning behind the Korean idiom 마음에도 없는 말을 하다. Literally the phrase means "to say something that is not even in your heart" and would be used in a situation when you compliment someone without meaning it, or when someone offers you help without truly wanting to help.

A: 은경 씨, 오늘 그럼 야근해야 하는 거예요?

B: 어쩔 수 없죠. 퇴근하세요?

A: 네. 저도 남아서 도와주고 싶은데 오늘은 저도 약속이 있어서요.

B: 마음에도 없는 말 하지 말고 빨리 퇴근하세요.

A: Eun-gyeong. Do you have to work overtime then?

B: I have no choice. Are you leaving?

A: Yes. I would like to stay and help you, but I have to be somewhere.

B: Don't say what you don't mean and just go.

A: 오늘 진짜 스트레스 받는다. 오늘 약속 있어? 술이나 한잔 하자.

B: 오늘? 나 오늘 혜진 씨랑 만나기로 했는데. 같이 만날까?

A: 됐어. 마음에도 없는 말 하지 말고 빨리 데이트나 가.

B: 미안하다. 내일 마시자.

A: I'm so stressed out today. Do you have to go somewhere today? Let's have a drink or something.

B: Today? I am supposed to meet Hyejin today. Do you want to go together?

A: Forget it. I know you don't even mean it. Go enjoy your date.

B: Sorry. Let's have a drink tomorrow.

CHAPTER. 76

띄우다 = to float something;
to fly something
-아/어/여 주다 = to do something for someone

띄워 주다
[tti-wo ju-da]

LITERAL TRANSLATION:
to float or fly something for someone

ACTUAL USAGE:
to flatter; to praise someone a lot

띄워 주다 is hardly used for its literal meaning, as it's highly unlikely that you can fly or float someone. However, as an idiomatic expression, it means "to praise someone a lot" or "to sing one's praise." 띄워 주다 is similar to 비행기 태우다, and can be used in the same situation, but 띄워 주다 is used more often just to simply flatter someone, not to exaggerate or to intentionally inflate a person's ego. When using 띄워 주다, the person's name or term you use to address that person comes before the expression, "지영이를 띄워 주다" or "동생을 띄워 주다."

A: 준하 씨 오늘 왜 이렇게 멋져요?

　　B: 왜요? 갑자기 왜 칭찬을 해요?

A: 머리 스타일 바꿨어요? 옷 새로 샀어요?

　　B: 갑자기 띄워 주는 게 수상한데요? 부탁할 거 있어요?

A: Junha, why do you look so awesome today?

*　　B: Why? Why are you praising me suddenly?*

A: Did you change your hairstyle? Did you get new clothes?

*　　B: It's strange that you are suddenly praising me. Is there something you want to ask me as a favor?*

A: 상희 씨는 얼굴만 예쁜지 알았는데 요리 솜씨도 좋네요.

　　B: 저녁 맛있었어요?

A: 정말 맛있었어요. 진짜 못하는 게 없네요. 남자들한테 인기 많겠어요.

　　B: 자꾸 띄워 주지만 말고 소개팅이라도 좀 시켜 주세요.

A: Sang-hee, I thought you were only pretty, but you are also good at cooking.

*　　B: Was the dinner delicious?*

A: It was really delicious. You really are good at everything. You must be popular among guys.

*　　B: Stop just praising me like that and just hook me up with a guy.*

CHAPTER. 77

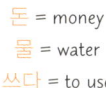

돈 = money
물 = water
쓰다 = to use

돈을 물 쓰듯 하다

[**do-neul mul sseu-deut ha-da**]

LITERAL TRANSLATION:

to spend money like one uses water

ACTUAL USAGE:

to spend money freely; to carelessly spend money; to squander money away

Depending on where you are in the world, water is used every day: to bathe, drink, wash dishes and clothes, and cook with. Now, imagine that water has turned into money. Watch as all that money goes down the drain like water! When a person is spending outside of his/her means and wasting money or "throwing money down the drain," this is referred to as "돈을 물 쓰듯 하다."

A: 월급이 들어오면 카드 값으로 다 나가.

　　B: 전부 다?

A: 응. 이상해.

　　B: 뭐가 이상해? 돈을 물 쓰듯 하니까 그렇지.

A: When my salary comes in, all of it goes out as a credit card payment.

　　B: All of it?

A: Yeah. It's strange.

　　B: What's strange? You are spending money too easily, that's why.

A: 너 또 가방 샀어? 가방이 도대체 몇 개야?

　　B: 몇 개 안 돼. 한정판으로 나왔는데 안 살 수가 없잖아.

A: 너 그렇게 돈을 물 쓰듯 해서 어떻게 시집가려고 하니?

　　B: 걱정 마. 저금도 하고 있어. 진짜야.

A: Did you buy another bag? How many bags do you have?

　　B: Not so many. This came out as a limited edition, and I couldn't pass it up.

A: If you keep spending money easily like that, how are you going to get married?

　　B: Don't worry. I'm also saving money. For real.

CHAPTER. 78

더위 = heat
먹다 = to eat

더위를 먹다
[deo-wi-reul meok-tta]

LITERAL TRANSLATION:
to eat the heat

ACTUAL USAGE:
to feel sick because of the heat
in the summer

In Korean, when you "eat the heat," it means that you feel sick or are ill because of the hot weather during the summer months. Even if you are not physically ill, being drained of energy because of the heat can cause a lack of motivation and/or appetite. This expression is not used with 추위 (cold) (See 추위를 타다).

A: 오늘 진짜 덥다.

B: 그치? 너무 더워서 더위 먹을 것 같아.

A: 정말. 우리 시원한 거라도 사 먹자.

A: It's really hot today.

B: Right? It's so hot that I will get sick.

A: Yeah. We should get something cold to eat

A: 나 오늘 중기 씨한테 고백할 거야.

B: 뭐? 너 더위 먹었어?

A: 왜? 중기 씨도 날 좋아하고 있을 수도 있어.

B: 소문 다 나고 차이고 싶은 거지?

A: I'm going to confess to Jung-gi today.

B: What? Have you gone crazy because of the heat?

A: Why? Jung-gi might be in love with me.

B: Do you want everybody to know about it and then get dumped?

CHAPTER. 79

간 = liver
기별 = notice; word; notification
안 = not
가다 = to go

간에 기별도 안 가다

[ga-ne gi-byeol-do an ga-da]

LITERAL TRANSLATION:
One's liver didn't get the message.

ACTUAL USAGE:
to barely begin to satisfy one's hunger;
the portion of food that one just ate was very small;
one is still hungry after eating something

When you eat something, but you still feel hungry, use the expression 간에 기별도 안 가다 to mean that you are still hungry and what you ate was not enough. "간에 기별도 안 가다" can be interpreted as "stomach is still growling" rather than taken literally as "liver didn't get the memo."

A: 아, 배고파. 뭐 먹을 거 없어?

B: 너 아까 점심 먹지 않았어?

A: 먹었어. 근데 양이 적어서 간에 기별도 안 갔어. 더 배고픈 것 같아.

A: I'm hungry. Is there anything to eat?

B: Didn't you have lunch earlier?

A: I did. But the amount was so small that I don't feel full at all. I think I'm even hungrier.

A: 크리스마스 파티 준비는 다 끝났어요?

B: 네. 다 끝났어요. 음식 준비도 드디어 끝났어요.

A: 음식이 이게 끝이에요? 100명이 오는데 간에 기별도 안 가겠어요.

B: 네? 50명 아니었어요?

A: Have you finished the preparations for the Christmas party?

B: Yes, it's all finished. The food has finally been prepared, too.

A: This is all the food we have? 100 people are coming and it's nowhere close to being enough.

B: Huh? Wasn't it 50 people?

CHAPTER. 80

상처 = a scar
주다 = to give

상처를 주다
[sang-cheo-reul ju-da]

LITERAL TRANSLATION:
to give a scar

ACTUAL USAGE:
to hurt someone
with one's words or behavior

The verb "**나다**" or "**내다**" is typically paired with the noun "**상처**" to mean "to physically harm something/someone and leave behind a scar." However, when "**상처**" is together with "**주다,**" it usually does not mean "to physically give someone a scar", but rather "to scar someone with words or behavior," similar to the English "to cut (someone) down."

A: 태호 씨 여자 친구 또 바뀐 거예요?

    B: 제가 좀 능력이 있잖아요. 이번 여자 친구는 모델이에요.

A: 자꾸 여자한테 상처 주면 나중에 벌 받아요.

A: Taeho, you have a new girlfriend again?

    B: You know I'm fully capable. This time, my girlfriend is a model.

A: If you keep breaking girls' hearts, it will all come back to you later.

A: 진짜 이해가 안 가요. 우리 팀 여직원은 무슨 말만 하면 울어요.

    B: 자꾸 상처 주는 말만 하니까 그러죠.

A: 상처 주는 말 한 적 없어요. 일을 제대로 못 하니까 바로 잡아 준 것뿐이에요.

A: I really don't get it. A female employee on my team cries whenever I say something to her.

    B: That's because you keep saying things that hurt her feelings.

A: I never said anything to hurt her feelings. She was not doing a good job, so I just corrected her mistakes.

CHAPTER. 81

눈 = eye
앞 = front
캄캄하다 = to be dark

눈앞이 캄캄하다
[nun a-pi kam-ka-ma-da]

LITERAL TRANSLATION:
to be dark in front of one's eyes

ACTUAL USAGE:
to not know what to do
after one hears bad news

In Korean, when you hear bad news and it feels like "everything goes black" to where you do not know what to do, "눈앞이 캄캄하다" is how you would accurately describe your feelings.

A: 수능이 벌써 100일 남았네. 준비 잘 돼 가는 거지?

B: 아니요. 눈앞이 캄캄해요.

A: 잘할 거야. 모의고사 점수도 좋았잖아.

B: 아휴...

A: The college entrance exam is already just 100 days away. The preparations are going well, right?

B: No. I feel hopeless.

A: You'll do fine. Your mock exam results were good, too.

B: (Sigh)

A: 오늘 초등학생들이랑 소풍 간다면서요.

B: 네. 제주도로 소풍 가요.

A: 제주도 정말 좋죠.

B: 제주도는 좋죠. 아휴... 초등학생들이랑 가야 하니까 문제죠. 눈앞이 캄캄해요.

A: I heard you were going on a picnic with elementary school students.

B: Yes. I'm going on a picnic to Jeju Island.

A: Jeju Island is great.

B: Jeju Island is great. (Sigh) But the problem is that I have to go there with elementary school students. I feel hopeless.

CHAPTER. 82

뜬구름 = floating cloud
잡다 = to catch; to grab

뜬구름 잡다
[tteun-gu-reum jap-tta]

LITERAL TRANSLATION:
to catch floating clouds

ACTUAL USAGE:
to try to chase a dream
that's unlikely to be fulfilled

뜬구름 잡다 refers to chasing dreams that are impossible to fulfill, just as if you were to try to catch a floating cloud, you will ultimately fail because it is impossible. A similar English expression is "to build castles in the air."

A: 택준 씨 사업 잘되나 봐요.

　　B: 왜요? 택준 씨가 그래요?

A: 네. 투자받는다고 하던데요?

　　B: 아니에요. 뜬구름 잡는 거예요.

A: Looks like Taekjun's business is going well.

　　B: Why? Did Taekjun say that?

A: Yeah. He said that he's getting investments [in his business].

　　B: No. He's just building castles in the air.

A: 요즘 뭐 하고 지내요?

　　B: 저 요즘 연기 학원 다니고 있어요. 여기서 1년만 배우면 영화에 출연시켜 준다고 했어요.

A: 네? 그 말을 믿어요? 뜬구름 잡는 거 아니에요?

A: What are you up to these days?

　　B: These day, I'm going to an acting school. They said that if I learn from there for a year, they will put me in a movie.

A: What? And you believe that? Aren't they just building castles in the sky?

CHAPTER. 83

눈 = eye
깜짝하다 = to blink one's eyes
새 = 사이 = gap; space;
during, while; relationship

눈 깜짝할 사이에
[nun kkam-jja-kal sa-i-e]

LITERAL TRANSLATION:

while blinking one's eyes

ACTUAL USAGE:

in the blink of an eye

Although "눈 깜짝할 사이에" literally means "while blinking one's eye," just as the English idiom "in the blink of an eye," this Korean idiom means something happens very quickly; within a short amount of time, or you feel the time has passed very quickly.

A: 내가 아까 사다 놓은 과자 어디 갔어?
　　B: 다 먹었지.
A: 벌써?
　　B: 그럼 애들이 셋이나 되는데. 눈 깜짝할 사이에 다 없어졌어.

A: Where is the snack that I bought earlier?
　　B: We ate it all.
A: Already?
　　B: Of course. We have three kids. It's all gone in a second.

A: 진희 씨 어디 갔어요?
　　B: 집에 갔어요.
A: 네? 벌써요? 나 진희 씨한테 할 말 있었는데.
　　B: 저도 할 말 있어서 가지 말라고 하려고 했는데 눈 깜짝할 사이에 가 버렸어요.

A: Where is Jinhee?
　　B: She went home.
A: What? Really? I have something to say to her.
　　B: I had something to say to her, too, so I was going to ask her not to leave, but she disappeared in a second.

CHAPTER. 84

말 = word(s); langauge;
what one says
안 = not
되다 = to become

말도 안 되다

[mal-do an doe-da]

LITERAL TRANSLATION:

to not become words;
to not form words

ACTUAL USAGE:

to be nonsense;
something is unbelievable or absurd.

"말이 되다" literally means "to become a word," but as an idiomatic expression, it means "to make sense." By negating 말이 되다 with 안 to create "말이 안 되다," it means that something doesn't make sense. The -도 in "말도 안 되다" emphasizes how absurd or unlikely something is to be true, meaning that "it's impossible," "I can't believe it," or "that's unbelieveable." If you watch Korean dramas or listen to K-pop, "말도 안 돼" is used often.

A: 콘테스트 1등 누구예요?

　　B: 동기 씨가 1등 했어요.

A: 진짜요? 말도 안 돼.

　　B: 저도 깜짝 놀랐어요.

A: Who came in first place in the contest?

　　B: Dong-gi came in first place.

A: Really? That's impossible.

　　B: I was surprised, too.

A: 말도 안 되는 일이 벌어졌어요.

　　B: 뭐요?

A: 만수 씨가 밥을 샀어요.

　　B: 진짜요? 만수 씨를 10년을 알았는데 밥 산 적 한 번도 없었어요.

A: Something impossible just happened.

　　B: What?

A: Mansu paid for the meal.

　　B: Really? I've known him for 10 years, but he's never paid for a meal.

CHAPTER. 85

분위기 = atmosphere; ambience
휩쓸리다 = to be swept

분위기에 휩쓸리다
[bu-nwi-gi-e hwip-sseul-li-da]

LITERAL TRANSLATION:
to be swept away by the atmosphere

ACTUAL USAGE:
to be caught up in the moment;
to do something that one wouldn't usually do
by being swept up by the atmosphere

221

If someone is caught up in the moment, that person tends to get carried away or do/ say things which are out of the ordinary. In Korean, this is referred to as "**분위기에 휩쓸리다,**" or "being swept away by the atmosphere." For example, you are at a baseball game and someone on the team you are cheering for scored a home run to tie the game. You are so excited that you turn to the stranger next to you and give him/her a hug. Following the awkward realization that you hugged a stranger, you can say, "**분위기에 휩쓸렸어요.**"

A: 두 분은 어떻게 사귀게 됐어요?

B: 원래 그냥 직장 동료였는데 월드컵 응원 갔다가 사귀게 됐어요.

A: 네? 어떻게 그래요?

B: 월드컵 응원하다가 한국이 이기고 있었거든요. 그 분위기에 휩쓸려서 사귀자고 했죠.

A: How did you two end up dating each other?

B: We were just coworkers at first, but we ended up dating after we went to cheer for a World Cup game.

A: What? How?

B: We were cheering together and Korea was winning. We were caught up in the moment and I asked her to date me.

A: 여보, 어제 친구들 만나서 술값을 다 당신이 냈어요?

B: 아, 어쩔 수가 없었어.

A: 왜 자꾸 분위기에 휩쓸려서 돈을 다 내는 거예요?

B: 미안해. 나 승진해서 모인 자리라서 어쩔 수가 없었어.

A: Honey, did you pay for all the drinks when you met your friends last night?

B: I couldn't help it.

A: Why do you always get caught up in the moment and pay for everything?

B: I'm sorry. They were there because of my promotion, so I had no choice.

CHAPTER. 86

뼈 = bone
빠지다 = to fall out/off
일하다 = to work

뼈 빠지게 일하다
[ppyeo ppa-ji-ge i-ra-da]

LITERAL TRANSLATION:

to work until your bones fall off

ACTUAL USAGE:

to work very hard

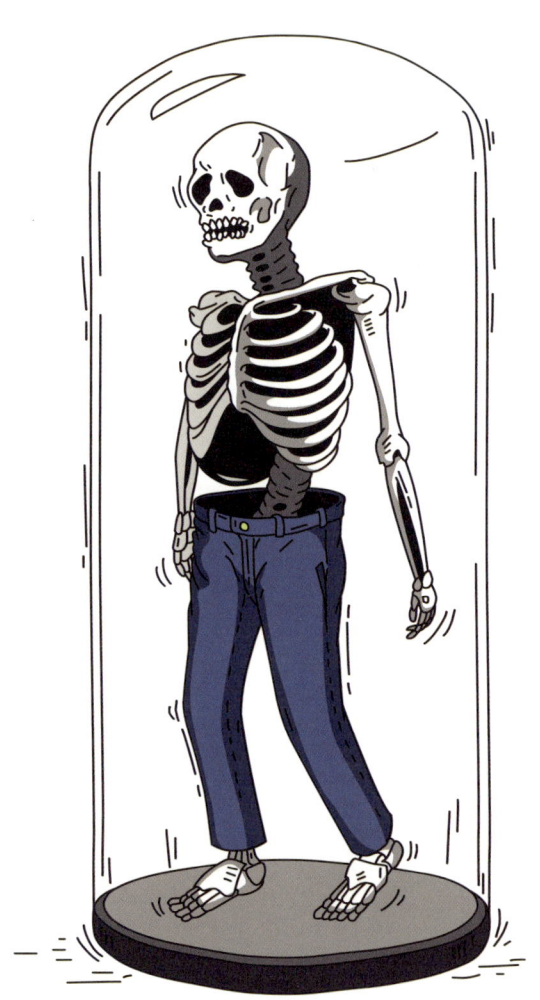

When you are working really, really hard, for instance, to support you family or pay off your debts, you are "뼈 빠지게 일하다." This expression really emits the feeling that you are sacrificing nearly everything in order to achieve a personal goal or for the sake of others, even if it's physically or mentally taxing. A similar English idiom is "to work your tail off."

A: 애들이 미국에 유학 가고 싶다고 하네요.

B: 부인은요? 부인도 같이 가고요?

A: 애들만 보내기 걱정된다고 같이 가고 싶어 해요.

B: 그냥 한국에 있으라고 해요. 혼자 한국에서 뼈 빠지게 일해서 유학 자금 보내면 무슨 소용이 있어요. 가족은 함께 해야죠.

A: My kids want to go study abroad in the USA.

B: What about your wife? She wants to go, too?

A: She also wants to go because she'll be worried about just letting the kids go.

B: Tell them to just stay in Korea. What's the point if you work your tail off by yourself here in Korea and send them money for studying? A family needs to be together.

A: 뼈 빠지게 하루 종일 일해도 다 소용없어.

B: 무슨 일 있어?

A: 우리 회사에 사장님 친척 있잖아? 그 사람 벌써 부장이래.

B: 벌써? 들어온 지 한 달밖에 안 된 거 아냐?

A: 맞아.

A: Even if I work my tail off, it's all pointless.

B: What's wrong?

A: There's this relative of the boss working at my company, right? He's already a manager now.

B: Already? Didn't he enter a month ago?

A: That's right.

CHAPTER. 87

생각 = thought; idea
짧다 = to be short

생각이 짧다
[saeng-ga-gi jjal-tta]

LITERAL TRANSLATION:
One's thought is short.

ACTUAL USAGE:
to act/speak without thinking;
to be unintentionally inconsiderate

If someone speaks or acts without thinking, that person can be described as "생각이 짧다," meaning that their thought process was short or non-existent, not literally that their thoughts are short. Even if a person is unintentionally rude because he/she did not think things through, and he/she regrettably said or did something, this idiom can still be used to describe that person.

A: 아, 내가 생각이 짧았어.

    B: 왜?

A: 사장님한테 잘 보이려고 와인을 사 갔는데 사장님이 와인은 안 드신다고 하시네.

A: That was a mistake.

    B. Why?

A: I wanted to win the boss' favor, so I bought some wine for him, but he says he doesn't drink wine.

A: 너 왜 이렇게 생각이 짧아?

    B: 왜? 무슨 말이야?

A: 내가 어제 한 얘기 수정이한테 말했다며.

    B: 아, 비밀이었어? 난 몰랐어.

A: Why are you so thoughtless?

    B: Why? What do you mean?

A: I heard you told Sujeong what I told you yesterday.

    B: Was that a secret? I didn't know.

CHAPTER. 88

발 = foot
디디다 = to step on something
틈 = crack; gap;
(spare) time; chance

발 디딜 틈이 없다
[bal di-dil teu-mi eop-tta]

LITERAL TRANSLATION:
to not have a place to put one's foot down

ACTUAL USAGE:
to be very crowded

If you have ever attended a sold-out concert or been in an extremely crowded subway, it might feel as if your feet can't even touch the ground because there are so many people. 발 디딜 틈이 없다 applies to any type of situation such as this, where it is extremely crowded, like the 홍대 area on a Friday night during the summer.

A: 어제 민서 씨네 레스토랑 오픈했다면서요?

B: 네. 어제 왜 안 왔어요?

A: 너무 바빴어요. 사람 많았어요?

B: 네. 발 디딜 틈이 없었어요.

A: Minseo, I heard your restaurant opened yesterday.

B: Yes. Why didn't you come yesterday?

A: I was too busy. Were there a lot of people?

B: Yes. It was packed.

A: 집에 뭐 타고 가요?

B: 전 버스 타고 가요. 수희 씨는요?

A: 저는 지하철 타고 가요. 그런데 우리 같은 동네 살지 않아요?

B: 이 시간에 지하철 타면 발 디딜 틈이 없어요. 전 버스가 낫더라고요.

A: How are you going home?

B: I'm taking the bus. What about you, Suhee?

A: I'm taking the subway. But, don't we live in the same neighborhood?

B: If you take the subway around this time, it's packed. I find the bus better.

CHAPTER. 89

간 = liver
콩알 = a bean

간이 콩알만 해지다
[ga-ni kong-al-man hae-ji-da]

LITERAL TRANSLATION:
One's liver shrinks down
to the size of a bean.

ACTUAL USAGE:
to feel scared

In Korean, **간이 콩알만 해지다** refers to being so startled by something all of a sudden that your liver shrinks to the size of a bean. This expression is not used to describe something which you are afraid of on a day-to-day basis, such as ghosts. However, if you are normally afraid of ghosts, and one day you actually see one, you can say "**간이 콩알만 해졌다!**"

A: 어제 사무실 분위기 정말 안 좋았어요.

    B: 어제요? 왜요?

A: 차장님이 재철 씨한테 화를 내는데 진짜 무서웠어요. 간이 콩알만 해지는 줄 알았어요.

    B: 차장님 원래 화 잘 안 내잖아요.

A: The atmosphere in the office was really bad yesterday.

    B: Yesterday? Why?

A: The deputy head of department got angry at Jaecheol and it was really scary. I was really scared.

    B: He normally doesn't get angry very often.

A: 영화 재미있게 봤어?

    B: 아니, 너무 무서웠어. 간이 콩알만 해졌어.

A: 공포 영화 본 거야?

    B: 공포 영화인 줄 몰랐어.

A: Did you enjoy the movie?

    B: No, it was so scary. I was terrified.

A: Did you watch a horror movie?

    B: I didn't know it was a horror movie.

CHAPTER. 90

깨 = sesame
쏟아지다 = something pours (out of)

깨가 쏟아지다

[kkae-ga sso-da-ji-da]

LITERAL TRANSLATION:
to pour out/gush sesame seeds

ACTUAL USAGE:
to live happily; a couple is very happy with each other
and is having a sweet time together

The story behind this idiom is that when sesame seeds are harvested, you need to shake the plant for the seed pods to come out. Even with the lightest shake, the pods with the seeds will fall off easily. For that reason, harvesting sesame seeds is a fun, relaxing, and enjoyable experience for a lot of people. 깨가 쏟아지다 is typically used to describe a couple who is, like the experiencing of harvesting sesame seeds, very happy, fun, and relaxed.

A: 결혼하니까 좋아요?

　　B: 네. 너무 좋아요.

A: 사진 보니까 아주 깨가 쏟아지던데요.

A: Are you happy to be married?

　　B: Yes, I am very happy.

A: I saw your pictures and you look really happy.

A: 신영 씨 요즘 행복하겠어요?

　　B: 아휴, 요즘 남편이랑 맨날 싸워요.

A: 왜요? 깨가 쏟아지는 신혼에 왜 싸워요.

A: Sinyeong, are you happy these days?

　　B: (Sigh) I fight with my husband all the time these days.

A: Why? You are happy newlyweds. Why do you fight?

CHAPTER. 91

손꼽다 = to count on one's fingers
기다리다 = to wait

. . . . . .

손꼽아 기다리다
[son-kko-ba gi-da-ri-da]

LITERAL TRANSLATION:

to wait for something
while counting on one's fingers

ACTUAL USAGE:

to look forward to/wait
for something very eagerly

If you are very eagerly awaiting something, like attending a big event or going on vacation, you might cross off the days on a calendar or count down the days in anticipation on your fingers. Therefore, "손꼽아 기다리다" doesn't literally mean that you are "waiting while counting on one's fingers," but rather that you are looking forward to and are really excited about the upcoming big day.

A: 내일부터 휴가네요.

    B: 네. 휴가만 손꼽아 기다렸어요. 너무 좋아요.

A: 어디 놀러 가요?

    B: 아니요. 집에서 잠만 잘 거예요.

A: So, you're on vacation starting tomorrow.

    B: Yes. I've been waiting forever for the vacation. I'm so excited.

A: Are you going somewhere?

    B: No. I'm going to stay at home and just sleep.

A: 내일이 빨리 왔으면 좋겠어요.

    B: 왜요?

A: 내일 제가 좋아하는 게임의 새 버전이 나오는 날이거든요. 한 달 내내 이날만 손꼽아 기다렸어요.

A: I can't wait for tomorrow.

    B: Why?

A: Tomorrow is the day that the new version of my favorite game is released. I've really been looking forward to this day the entire month.

CHAPTER. 92

날개 = wing
돋치다 = to fledge
팔리다 = to be sold

날개 돋친 듯 팔리다
[nal-gae dot-chin deut pal-li-da]

LITERAL TRANSLATION:
to be sold as if wings are fledged

ACTUAL USAGE:
Something is selling like hot cakes.

When a young bird has grown into an adult bird and its feathers are full and beautiful, if being sold, the beautiful and full-fledged birds will sell better than younger birds. As an idiom, "날개 돋친 듯 팔리다" refers to products that sell well, such as ice cream on a hot summer day (아이스크림이 날개 돋친 듯 팔린다). A similar English idiom is "to sell like hot cakes."

A: 이번에 새로 나온 상품 잘 팔리는 거 같아요?
　　B: 나오자마자 날개 돋친 듯 팔리고 있어요.
A: 정말요? 축하해요.

A: Do you think the new product is selling well?
　　B: It's been selling like hot cakes as soon as it was launched.
A: Really? Congratulations.

A: 너무 속상해요.
　　B: 왜요?
A: 며칠 전에 신제품이 나왔는데 잘 안 팔리네요.
　　B: 나오자마자 날개 돋친 듯 팔릴 줄 알았어요? 조금 더 기다려 봐요. 홍보도 좀 더 해 보고요.

A: I'm so upset.
　　B: Why?
A: We had a new product come out a few days ago, but it's not selling well.
　　B: Did you think it would start selling like hot cakes right after release? Wait a little more and also do some more promotion.

날개 돋친 듯 팔리다

240

CHAPTER. 93

물거품 = foam/bubble (in the water)
되다 = to become

물거품이 되다
[mul-geo-pu-mi doe-da]

LITERAL TRANSLATION:
to become a bubble

ACTUAL USAGE:
One's hope gets crushed.

물거품 refers to the delicate foam or bubbles that form in water which can be reduced to nothing or popped. If a person's dreams or hopes are crushed, or his/her efforts are in vain, you can use the expression "물거품이 되다" to describe the situation. In English, you can say, "burst your/my bubble."

A: 아휴. 다시 해야겠다.

    B: 왜 그래?

A: 오전부터 문서 작업 하고 있었는데 컴퓨터가 그냥 꺼졌어.

    B: 저장 안 되고?

A: 응. 지금까지 한 거 전부 물거품 되어 버렸네...

A: (Sigh) I'll have to do it again.

    B: Why?

A: I've been working on this document since this morning and my computer just crashed.

    B: It wasn't saved?

A: No. Everything I've worked on so far all disappeared.

A: 부모님 여행 못 가신다고 하시네.

    B: 정말? 왜?

A: 아빠가 그때 휴가를 못 쓰게 되셨다고. 내가 한 달 동안 계획 짠 게 물거품이 되었어.

A: My parents say they can't go on a trip.

    B: Really? Why?

A: My father won't be able to use his vacation days at that time. All my planning for the past month is in vain.

CHAPTER. 94

바람 = wind
맞다 = to get hit

• • • •

바람맞다
[**ba-ram-mat-tta**]

LITERAL TRANSLATION:
to get hit by the wind

ACTUAL USAGE:
to get stood up

Imagine that you are standing outside when it's windy out and you are waiting for your date to show up. The only problem is that your date is a no-show. In this case, the wind is literally hitting you because you're waiting for someone who never shows up. An English phrase with equivalent meaning to "바람맞다" is "to be stood up."

A: 어제 데이트 잘했어요?

B: 바람맞았어요.

A: 네? 왜요? 둘이 잘 지내는 거 아니었어요?

B: 모르겠어요. 전화도 안 받아요.

A: Did you have a good date yesterday?

B: I was stood up.

A: What? Why? Weren't you two getting along well?

B: I don't know. She doesn't even pick up the phone.

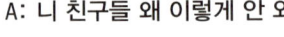

A: 니 친구들 왜 이렇게 안 와?

B: 조금만 기다려 봐. 금방 올 거야.

A: 벌써 30분이나 기다렸어. 우리 바람맞은 거 아냐?

B: 그럴 리가 없어. 전화 다시 해 볼게.

A: Why are your friends still not coming?

B: Just wait a little more. They'll be here soon.

A: We've already waited for 30 minutes. Are you sure we are not stood up?

B: That's impossible. I'll call them again.

CHAPTER. 95

갈수록 태산이다
[gal-su-rok tae-sa-ni-da]

LITERAL TRANSLATION:
The more one forges ahead,
the bigger the mountain gets.;
after a mountain is another mountain

ACTUAL USAGE:
As life goes on,
each problem seems more insurmountable
than the one before it.

The Sino-Korean letter 태 (太) means "to be huge"; therefore, the word "태산" is "a huge mountain," like Mount Kilimanjaro or Mount Everest. As you go through life, there will always be obstacles, and 갈수록 태산이다 is used to describe the problems in life that you face which seem to get bigger and tougher as you follow your life path.

A: 길을 잃은 것 같아요.
　B: 산속이라 핸드폰도 안 돼요.
A: 이제 비까지 오네요.
　B: 갈수록 태산이네요.

A: I think we're lost.
　B: Since we're in the mountain, the phone is not working either.
A: And it's raining, too.
　B: Things just keep getting worse.

A: 갈수록 태산이네요. 이 컴퓨터도 안 켜져요.
　B: 언제까지 해야 되는데요?
A: 오늘까지 끝내야 돼요.

A: It's getting worse. This computer won't turn on either.
　B: When do you have to finish it by?
A: I have to finish it by today.

CHAPTER. 96

꿀 = honey
먹다 = to eat; to drink
벙어리 = speech-impaired person; mute

꿀 먹은 벙어리
[kkul meo-geun beong-eo-ri]

LITERAL TRANSLATION:
a mute who has eaten honey

ACTUAL USAGE:
someone who does not say anything

벙어리 is an archaic way to refer to someone who cannot speak. If you use this word by itself these days, it can be offensive. Used in the idiom "꿀 먹은 벙어리," however, it is not. Since "꿀" means "honey," and "먹다" means "to eat," this expression refers to a person who normally speaks with no problem, but has chosen not to speak in certain situations. For example, if a student stops speaking when he/she is scolded, you can say he/she is "꿀 먹은 벙어리." An English idiom with a similar meaning is "cat got your tongue?"

A: 은영 씨, 왜 울어요? 무슨 일 있대요?
　　B: 모르겠어요.
A: 가서 한 번 물어봐요.
　　B: 이미 물어봤는데 대답을 안 해요. 꿀 먹은 벙어리예요.

A: Why is Eunyeong crying? Did something happen?
　　B: I don't know.
A: Go ask her.
　　B: I already did, but she won't answer. She's not talking.

A: 경수야 학교에서 친구들이 괴롭히니?
　　B: 아니요.
A: 그럼 선생님이 때린 거야? 왜 이렇게 꿀 먹은 벙어리처럼 말을 안 해. 얼굴에 멍이 시퍼렇게 들었잖아.

A: Kyeongsu, are your classmates bullying you?
　　B: No.
A: Then did your teacher hit you? Why won't you talk? You have a dark bruise on your face.

CHAPTER. 97

속다 = to get fooled;
to get tricked; to be deceived
셈 치다 = to suppose;
to assume; to grant (that)

속는 셈 치고
[song-neun sem chi-go]

LITERAL TRANSLATION:
to assume oneself is being decieved;
to let the other person fool you

ACTUAL USAGE:
to have nothing to lose;
to give the benefit of the doubt

속는 셈 치다 is used to describe a situation when you are about to do something that you are doubting. Basically you are taking a risk because you have nothing to lose, are deceiving yourself, or you are giving someone the benefit of the doubt even if you are a bit uneasy. Self-deception occurs when you say something to yourself such as "속는 셈 치고" (let's pretend I'm being deceived and just do this, even if I am unsure). When you give someone the benefit of the doubt, you can say, "속는 셈 치고 다시 한 번 믿어 볼게요" (I'm a bit skeptical about doing this, but I'm just pretending to be deceived and I will believe you one more time).

A: 요즘 하는 일마다 다 잘 안되죠?
　　B: 힘들어 죽겠어요.
A: 속는 셈 치고 이거 하나 사서 집에 붙여 놔요.
　　B: 전 부적은 안 믿어요.

A: Everything you do these days is not working out, right?
　　B: It's driving me crazy.
A: Buy one of these and put it on the wall in your house. You have nothing to lose.
　　B: I don't believe in charms.

A: 친구가 자꾸 소개팅시켜 준다네.
　　B: 부럽다. 하지 왜 안 해?
A: 난 소개팅 자리 불편하더라. 예쁘다는데 그 말을 어떻게 믿어.
　　B: 속는 셈 치고 한 번 나가 봐. 진짜 예쁠 수도 있잖아.

A: My friend keeps saying he'll set me up for a blind date.
　　B: I'm jealous. Why are you not doing it?
A: I usually find blind dates uncomfortable. He says she's pretty but how can I trust him?
　　B: You have nothing to lose. She might be actually pretty.

CHAPTER. 98

일 = work; thing; occasion; stuff
꼬이다 = to be entangled; to be twisted •

일이 꼬이다
[**i-ri kko-i-da**]

LITERAL TRANSLATION:

to twist things up

ACTUAL USAGE:

Things don't go well as one planned.

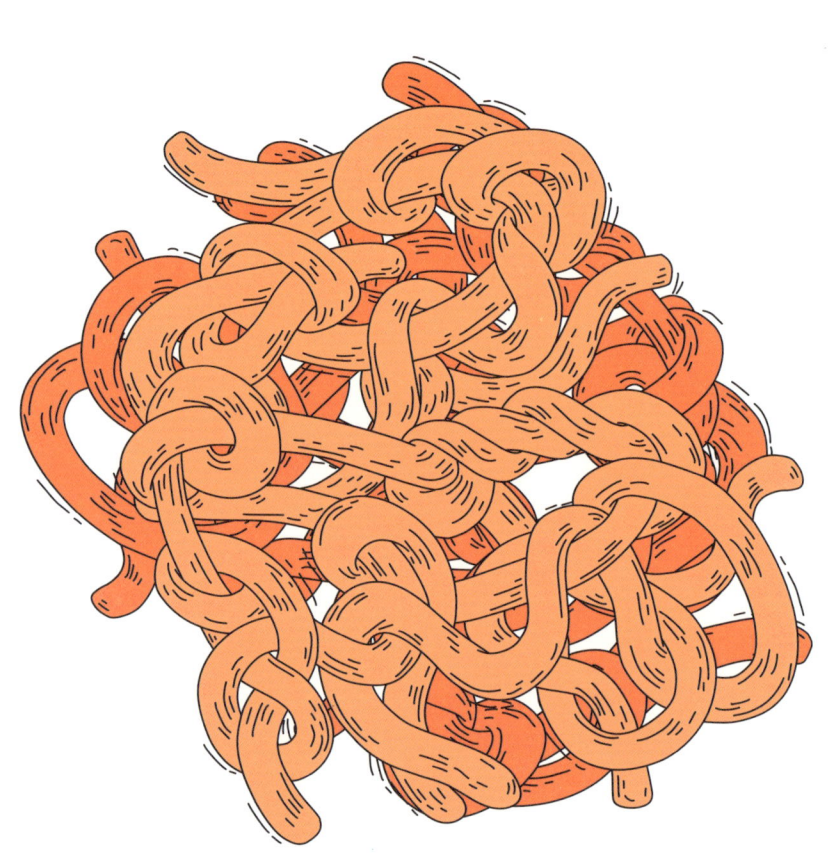

The word 일 can be translate to English in many different ways, but here it refers to the how things are turning out. Imagine that you are throwing a surprise party for a friend, and you planned the surprise around having a cake with candles lit when your friend arrived. However, the person bringing the cake says they will show up late, which is going to mess things up. Since things are not going well or as you planned, you can say "일이 꼬이다."

A: 오늘도 야근해?

　　B: 야근해야 할 것 같아.

A: 오늘은 같이 저녁 먹기로 했잖아.

　　B: 진짜 미안해. 일이 다 꼬여서 꼭 야근을 해야 해.

A: Are you working overtime again today?

　　B: I think I'll have to work overtime.

A: We were going to have dinner together.

　　B: I'm so sorry. Things went awry and I have to work overtime.

A: 아, 일이 꼬여도 이렇게 꼬일 수가 있지?

　　B: 왜? 무슨 일이야?

A: 어제 독서실 안 가고 친구들이랑 놀았거든. 근데 우리가 간 식당 주인이 엄마 친구래.

　　B: 엄마한테 걸렸어?

A: 엄마한테 걸리고 핸드폰도 뺏겼어.

A: How can things go wrong in so many ways?

　　B: Why? What happened?

A: I skipped going to the study room and hung out with friends. But, it turns out that the owner of the restaurant we went to is my mother's friend.

　　B: Did you get caught by your mother?

A: I got busted by mom and she also took my phone.

255

CHAPTER. 99

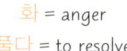
화 = anger
풀다 = to resolve

화풀이하다

[**hwa-pu-ri-ha-da**]

LITERAL TRANSLATION:

to resolve one's anger

ACTUAL USAGE:

to vent one's anger to someone who's not guilty
for the anger

When you use the expression "화풀이하다" in Korean, it not only means "to resolve your anger," but more specifically, venting to someone or something who did not cause you to anger. For example, if you punch your pillow when you are angry, your pillow is on the receiving end of your 화풀이.

A: 오늘 진짜 짜증 나는데 너까지 나한테 왜 그래?

B: 내가 뭘?

A: 왜 늦게 와. 5분이나 기다렸잖아.

B: 미안해. 근데 왜 나한테 화풀이야. 겨우 5분 늦었는데.

A: I'm already having a bad day. Why do you have to make it worse?

B: What did I do?

A: Why were you late? I waited for as long as five minutes.

B: I'm sorry. But, why are you taking it out on me? I was just five minutes late.

A: 김승윤! 걸리기만 해 봐라!

B: 왜? 승윤이가 또 뭐 잘못했어?

A: 아후, 내 지갑에서 돈 가져갔어. 너도 조심해. 내 지갑에서 돈 가져가기만 해 봐.

B: 난 아무 잘못 없어. 나한테 화풀이하지 말고 승윤이나 잡아.

A: Seung-yun Kim! Once I catch you, you're in big trouble!

B: Why? What did Seung-yun did wrong again?

A: He took money from my wallet. You should be careful, too. You take money from my wallet and I will...

B: I didn't do anything. Don't take it out on me and just go catch Seung-yun.

CHAPTER. 100

모르다 = to not know
약 = medicine

· · ·
모르는 게 약이다
[mo-reu-neun ge ya-gi-da]

LITERAL TRANSLATION:
Not knowing (something) is the medicine.

ACTUAL USAGE:
Ignorance is bliss.

모르는 게 약이다 is used to express that not knowing something might be better for you than knowing. In English, the expression "ignorance is bliss" has the same meaning as "모르는 게 약이다."

A: 여자들 마음은 진짜 알다가도 모르겠어.

B: 여자들 아주 단순한데?

A: 단순하긴. 마음을 읽을 수 있으면 얼마나 좋을까? 모든 여자들이 나를 좋아하고 있을 수도 있잖아.

B: 아휴... 모르는 게 약이다.

A: Sometimes I feel like I understand girls, but then again, I really don't understand them.

B: Girls are very simple.

A: Simple? No way. How nice would it be if I could read minds?! All girls might be in love with me.

B: (Sigh) Ignorance is bliss.

A: 진수 씨 요즘 소문이 안 좋던데요?

B: 왜요? 착하고 성실한 사람인데.

A: 항상 소문내고 다니는 현진 씨한테 잘못 보인 게 분명해요.

B: 진수 씨도 이 사실을 알아요?

A: 아니요. 모르는 게 약이에요.

A: Lately there are some bad rumors about Jinsu.

B: Why? He's a nice guy and he works hard.

A: I'm sure he made Hyeonjin upset. Hyeonjin always spreads rumors.

B: Does Jinsu know about this?

A: No. Ignorance is bliss.